No one else

can match the effectiveness, the simplicity,

SPECTRUM READING SERIES

Students gain meaningful practice— independently

With the SPECTRUM READING SERIES students not only get the practice they need in essential reading skills, they also enjoy being able to do it on their own.

In grades one through six, each lesson features an illustrated story followed by exercises in comprehension and basic reading skills. Because the same format is used consistently throughout, your students will have little trouble doing the lessons independently. And each two-page lesson can be finished easily in one class period.

Students develop and refine key reading skills.

- **Comprehension** exercises help students go beyond understanding of facts and details to drawing conclusions, predicting outcomes, identifying cause and effect, and developing other higher level comprehension skills.
- **Vocabulary development** builds on words from the reading selections. In addition to learning synonyms, antonyms, and words with multiple meanings, students develop sight vocabulary and learn to use context as a clue for meaning.
- **Decoding** exercises refine students' abilities to "attack" and understand new reading words.
- **Study skills** are developed by helping students apply their reading skills to new tasks, such as using reference materials, reading graphs, and applying other everyday life skills.

Reading selections captivate and motivate.

Students get their best reading practice by actually reading. That's why the selections in the SPECTRUM READING SERIES, in addition to offering practice in skills, also motivate students to read—just for fun.

Students quickly become friends with the characters in these entertaining stories. And they enjoy new levels of reading success—thanks in part to carefully controlled vocabulary and readability as well as beautiful illustrations.

The program adapts completely to any teaching situation.

The SPECTRUM READING SERIES can be used in many different ways.

- For the whole class . . . for intensive reinforcement of reading skills or to supplement a basal reading program.
- For reading groups . . . to provide skills practice at the appropriate levels.
- For individual use . . . to help build a completely individualized program.
- For at-home practice . . . to expand on skills learned in the classroom.

Index of Skills for *Reading Grade 6*

Numerals indicate the exercise pages on which these skills appear.

Knowing the Words

Working with Words

Reading and Thinking

Learning to Study

SPECTRUM READING
Grade 6

Table of Contents

A New Pilot

Read to find out if Charlie will be able to get along with a new pilot.

1   "I knew you'd find someone else," Charlie moaned. "But flying just won't be the same without Suzanne."

2   "Now, wait a minute," explained Howard, the cargo manager of a midwest cargo center. "Your new copilot is really good. She's flown since she was sixteen. She's been a flight instructor, and besides she's flown some of our smaller airplanes in Jacksonville and has done a whale of a job. We want to try her out up here."

3   "But nobody's going to be able to take Suzanne's place," Charlie said.

4   "Come on, Charlie. Don't prejudge her. You just might be surprised," Howard said as he smiled to himself.

5   Suddenly Amanda, the flight dispatcher, burst into the office.

6   "Howard, I thought you should know that we're having trouble with the landing gear on that plane from the South. The pilot just radioed that the fuel is running out. The fire crew is on alert, and they're ready to foam the runway if necessary. The pilot decided to land on the field adjoining the runway to avoid damaging the airplane. I'm headed there to see what is happening."

7   With that, Amanda ran from the room just as Howard answered the telephone, and Charlie ran to the window.

8   "I can see the plane from here," Charlie cried.

9   "They're going to land in the field," Howard declared while replacing the phone. "Let's hope that pilot knows what to do."

10   "Well, here goes," Charlie said as he unconsciously held his breath.

11   Out of the sky, the big silver bird headed for the edge of the wet, grassy surface. Ever so gently it skimmed the top of the grass and then bounced as the fuselage made contact with the soft earth. Amazingly, it came smoothly to a stop, leaving a muddy trail behind it.

12   "Goodness, that was beautiful!" Charlie exhaled. "I've seen rougher landings with the landing gear down."

13   In the next moment, Howard and Charlie arrived at the field just as the pilot emerged from the cockpit.

14   "Terrific job, Pat!" Howard shouted.

15   "Pat?" Charlie cried.

16   "Charlie!" Pat cried out. "It's great to see you. I've been looking forward to flying with you, but I didn't expect to reintroduce myself under these circumstances."

17   "You know each other?" Howard asked.

18   "Of course," Charlie answered. "Pat helped me learn the ropes in that computer flight-training course we took. She's the best pilot I know."

19   "Well, Charlie, meet your new copilot. I certainly hope you don't have any trouble working with her," Howard chuckled.

20   "Not very likely," Charlie said ashamedly as he and Pat turned to inspect the plane.

Knowing the Words

Write the words from the story that have the meanings below.

1. assistant pilot _____ (Par. 2)

2. teacher _____ (Par. 2)

3. decide before knowing the facts _____ (Par. 4)

4. one who schedules airplane flights _____ (Par. 5)

5. next to _____ (Par. 6)

6. unaware _____ (Par. 10)

7. airplane body _____ (Par. 11)

8. area where the pilot sits _____ (Par. 13)

An **idiom** is a phrase that cannot be understood by the meaning of its words. The phrase *break the ice* is an idiom. It means "to start a conversation." Find the phrases that are idioms in the story and write them.

9. _____ (Par. 2)

10. _____ (Par. 18)

Learning to Study

Dictionary entry words appear in dark print and are divided by spaces. These spaces show where the words can be divided at the end of a line of writing. Write the words below in syllables and in alphabetical order as they would appear as entries.

| copilot | fuselage | instructor |
| cockpit | prejudge | dispatcher |

1. _____   4. _____
2. _____   5. _____
3. _____   6. _____

Reading and Thinking

1. Check each word or phrase that describes Charlie in the story.

   ____ excitable

   ____ respects Pat

   ____ shy

2. Check each word or phrase that describes Pat in this story.

   ____ capable

   ____ athletic

   ____ loves flying

3. Check the most likely outcome of this story.

   ____ Pat will resent Charlie.

   ____ Pat and Charlie will get along.

   ____ Charlie will resent Pat.

Working with Words

A **suffix** is a letter or group of letters added to the end of a word to change the word's meaning or part of speech. The suffix **-ly** usually means "in a certain way." Write the words from the story that have the suffix **-ly** and that are formed from these base words.

1. real _____ (Par. 2)

2. sudden _____ (Par. 5)

3. unconscious _____ (Par. 10)

4. gentle _____ (Par. 11)

5. amaze _____ (Par. 11)

6. smooth _____ (Par. 11)

7. certain _____ (Par. 19)

8. like _____ (Par. 20)

9. ashamed _____ (Par. 20)

Anything Flies

Read to find out what types of cargo are shipped by air.

1 "If you had told me ten years ago when I took that computer course that we'd be flying together, I wouldn't have believed it," Charlie said while waiting to taxi to the runway.

2 "Hey," Pat replied, "we've done just fine these last three years. There really has been a lot of water under the bridge, though, hasn't there?"

3 Pat glanced back at the cargo bay of the Vista. It was like the fuselage of a huge passenger plane, except that it had no seats, windows, or anything except racks and stacks of containers. This time they were filled with roses that Pat and Charlie were taking to New Jersey from Oregon.

4 "Our cargo hasn't always smelled this sweet," laughed Pat. She thought of the trip they took with some of the creatures from the Columbus Zoo. What a flight that was! Both she and Charlie were terrified when the zoo employees couldn't find one of the poisonous snakes. Charlie was sure they would find it in their luggage. Luckily, Riva, the zoo manager, found that it was safe in its mislabeled crate.

5 The Vista had flown a wide variety of goods all over the world with Pat and Charlie at the helm. They had flown computer chips to Asia, plants from Brazil, and heavy trucks and cars from Europe. They had even flown racehorses from the Middle East to Kentucky.

6 Their air cargo list was nearly endless. They had shipped medicine, clothes, mail, hazardous materials, freezers, and car parts. They had also carried books and newspapers that were ready for sale not long after the ink was dry.

7 "In all this time, we've lost only one load," said Charlie. "Remember when we had the misfortune of being snowed in for three days in Denver with those twenty tons of vegetables? What a smell that was when we unloaded in Dallas! If we had been smarter, we would have set up the world's biggest salad bar when we had the chance."

8 "We've lost only one load, but we haven't always been punctual," Pat admitted. "Some people have had to wait a long time for their payroll checks."

9 "They could have waited a lot longer. Those checks could have been shipped by truck or train," Charlie responded.

10 "That's true," Pat agreed. "I know that the fruits and vegetables we transport can be made available to consumers in less than twenty-four hours from the time of harvest. Before cargo planes, produce had to be picked when it was still green. If not, it would spoil on the way.

11 "You know, though," Pat continued, "I don't think we've ever been more careful than when we transported those paintings from the Louvre Museum to Washington."

12 "You can't exactly repaint those pictures," Charlie added. "Yes, I guess I did a pretty good job of training you."

13 "Isn't it the other way around?" Pat said.

14 Charlie just laughed as the Vista headed down the runway to the waiting sky.

Knowing the Words

Write the words from the story that have the meanings below.

1. baggage _____
   (Par. 4)

2. head _____
   (Par. 5)

3. dangerous _____
   (Par. 6)

4. prompt _____
   (Par. 8)

5. buyers _____
   (Par. 10)

6. carried _____
   (Par. 11)

7. Find the **idiom** in the story and write it on the first line. Write the meaning of the idiom on the second line.

   _____
   (Par. 2)

   _____

Learning to Study

Dictionary definitions, or meanings, are most often short phrases, but they can also be single words. Find the entry words below in a dictionary. Then write the definitions that relate to air travel.

1. taxi _____

   _____

2. runway _____

   _____

3. cargo _____

   _____

4. container _____

   _____

5. bay _____

   _____

Reading and Thinking

1. Check the word that best describes Pat when she says, "We haven't always been punctual."

   ____ lazy

   ____ honest

   ____ early

2. Check the sentence that best expresses the main idea of this story.

   ____ A snake was lost in flight.

   ____ Pat and Charlie are friends.

   ____ Cargo planes ship a variety of goods.

3. Based on what you read in this story, check the words that describe the Vista.

   ____ huge   ____ modern

   ____ fast   ____ dark inside

Write the word that best completes each sentence.

4. The control tower is _____ the hangar.

   connecting   adjoining   transporting

5. The _____ is the body of an airplane.

   fuselage   cockpit   hangar

Working with Words

A **prefix** is a letter or a group of letters added to the beginning of a word to change its meaning. The prefix **mis-** means "badly" or "wrongly." Add the prefix **mis-** to these words.

1. labeled _____

2. fortune _____

3. behave _____

4. place _____

First Flight

Read to find out about Pat's first flight.

1   "The first time I ever flew in a plane was when I was in the sixth grade," Pat explained to Charlie as they were cruising at an altitude of thirty thousand feet. "Even though I've flown a thousand times since then, I'll never forget that thrill.

2   "I was on my way to visit my cousins in Maine for two weeks. I was so excited about the trip that I packed my luggage a month in advance. On the day of the flight, I made sure we got to the airport extra early.

3   "When we got to the terminal, we went directly to the ticket counter. We bought my ticket and checked my luggage. I watched in amazement as my bags traveled away on a conveyor belt. Behind the counter was the schedule. I was excited to find my plane's departure time and gate number.

4   "Even though it was before the days of covered walkways and electronic inspection gates, it all seemed so new to me. I sat down in the waiting area in a chair that had a pay TV attached. Then I walked by some gift shops and a few small restaurants.

5   "From the terminal window, I watched in awe as the planes landed and took off. One of the flight attendants showed me my plane when it came down the taxiway to the loading ramp. I watched as the ground crew rolled the stairway into place. Suddenly the door opened, and people began streaming out. An empty baggage trailer drove up, and two people began to unload the luggage from the plane. This was right before a trailer loaded with the new luggage arrived. A food car came next, and the precooked food trays were loaded into the cabin. Finally a fuel tank drove up and refueled the airplane. All this was so new to me.

6   "When it was time to board, I suddenly realized I would be leaving my family. I'd been so excited about my trip, I hadn't thought about leaving them. Walking up the stairway, I had to hold back some tears when I saw my parents waving good-bye.

7   "Stepping through the doorway, I caught my first glimpse of a cockpit. It looked fascinating with its panel of lights and controls. The flight attendant showed me to my window seat. I buckled my seatbelt, heard about the emergency exits, and found myself ready for takeoff.

8   "My first sight of land from the air was spectacular. What had been a familiar landscape was like a toy city. In the next minute, we were surrounded by a thick fog and then bright sunlight. I thought the clouds looked like puffs of cotton.

9   "The flight took three hours, but it seemed like only a few minutes when the pilot told us to fasten our seatbelts for landing. I had only just finished my dinner. I felt scared when the plane bounced as we touched the runway before the pilot applied the brakes.

10   "Walking down the stairway, I saw my cousins and aunt waving excitedly at the terminal window. When I finally reached them, all I could talk about was how thrilling my flight had been. I knew then and there that I was going to be a pilot."

Knowing the Words

Write the words from the story that have the meanings below.

1. transportation
   station   _____

(Par. 3)

2. moving carrier _____

(Par. 3)

3. paved area
   for loading planes _____

(Par. 5)

4. sensational _____

(Par. 8)

5. scenery _____

(Par. 8)

A **simile** is a figure of speech in which two unlike things are compared. Similes use the word *like* or *as*. Write the actual meaning of the similes from paragraph 8.

6. *landscape was like a toy city*

_____

7. *clouds looked like puffs of cotton*

_____

Working with Words

A **compound word** is formed by putting two or more words together to make a new word. Write the compound words from the story that are formed by adding to these words.

1. air _____

(Par. 2)

2. taxi _____

(Par. 5)

3. stair _____

(Par. 5)

4. seat _____

(Par. 7)

5. off _____

(Par. 7)

6. land _____

(Par. 8)

7. sun _____

(Par. 8)

8. run _____

(Par. 9)

Reading and Thinking

1. Number the events to show the order in which they happened in time.

   ____ Pat and Charlie were cruising at thirty thousand feet.

   ____ Pat watched her suitcases on the airport's conveyor belt.

   ____ Pat packed her suitcases.

   ____ Pat saw the cockpit.

   ____ Pat saw her cousin waving.

   ____ Pat saw her parents waving.

2. Authors write stories to inform, to entertain, or to persuade. Check the most likely reason the author had for writing this story.

   ____ to inform

   ____ to entertain

   ____ to persuade

3. Why did Pat pack her luggage a month before her trip? _____

_____

Learning to Study

Using this airline flight schedule and information from the story, write the following information about Pat's flight.

Flight Schedule				
Flight	Destination	Departing	Arriving	Gate
238	Newark, NJ	9:45 A.M.	1:00 P.M.	15
965	Toronto, ON	1:15 P.M.	5:45 P.M.	17
455	Bangor, ME	3:45 P.M.	7:01 P.M.	5

1. Gate Number _____

2. Flight Number _____

3. Departure Time _____

4. Arrival Time _____

5. Destination _____

Flying Solo

Read to find out what Charlie had to learn before his first solo flight.

1   "I've wanted to be a pilot ever since I can remember," Charlie told Pat on their way from the hangar. "My grandfather told me stories about some of the heroic pilots he knew during the war. Growing up in the Southwest, I knew many people who worked in gloomy silver mines. I wanted to be high above the earth, not underneath it.

2   "My aunt had a small plane that she kept at a tiny airport near us. She used to take me up in it, but never as much as I wanted. She never let me fly the plane.

3   "When I was just sixteen, I took my first flying lessons. During the very first lesson, my instructor let me fly the plane a little. It was scary and thrilling at the same time. Even though I had watched my aunt, I was confused by all the controls and by the communications from the control tower. On the ground, I had a hard time steering with my feet at the same time that I controlled the wheel and throttle with my hands.

4   "At the time, it seemed as if there was so much to learn. I had to work on taking off,

landing, and making turns. I had a lot of trouble with turns and slowing the plane without losing altitude.

5   "Before I knew how important they were, I was annoyed with all the preflight checks. At the time, I couldn't believe how much there was to do. I had to learn to inspect the flaps and hinges, check the fuel level, and make sure that no water had condensed in the gas tanks. My instructor made sure that I checked the engine for oil leaks, cracked hoses, and bird nests. After all that, there was more, including the landing gear, the tail assembly, and the lights. Once inside, I checked all the instruments and each step of the flight plan. Little did I know how easily I'd be able to do all this later on.

6   "I'll never forget my first solo flight. I was scared to death, but I didn't want anyone to realize it. My hands were blocks of ice as I climbed into the cockpit after completing my preflight check. When the control tower cleared me for takeoff, my heart became a rocket.

7   "Somehow the plane rose smoothly into the air. I was amazed at how quiet it was alone in the plane. I really did feel as if I owned the sky.

8   "It seemed as if it was only a few seconds before I had completed my tricky maneuvers. In the next minute, I began a descent. Before I knew it, I was taxiing to a stop. Suddenly I remembered that there were other people in the universe. My aunt and my instructor came running out to the plane to congratulate me.

9   "I guess that instructor did a pretty good job because I passed my written exam with flying colors. Then I logged enough solo hours to get my private pilot's license.

10   "You know, Pat, it's funny, but I still feel as excited about flying as I did on that first solo. I'm just a little less frightened."

Knowing the Words

Write the words from the story that have the meanings below.

1. lever that regulates the flow of fuel to an engine _____ (Par. 3)

2. height above the earth _____ (Par. 4)

3. parts put together _____ (Par. 5)

4. planned movements _____ (Par. 8)

5. downward movement _____ (Par. 8)

A **metaphor** is a figure of speech in which two unlike objects are compared directly. Unlike a simile, the word *like* or *as* is not used to make the comparison. Check the correct meaning of the metaphor, *my hands were blocks of ice*, from paragraph 6.

6. ____ I was nervous.

____ My hands had been replaced by large ice cubes.

Check the correct meaning of the metaphor, *my heart became a rocket*, in paragraph 6.

7. ____ My heart turned into a rocket.

____ I was frightened.

Working with Words

The suffix **-y** can mean "full of" or "like." Write the words from the story that have the suffix **-y** and are formed from these base words.

1. scare _____ (Par. 3)

2. assemble _____ (Par. 5)

Write the words that have the suffix **-y** and the meanings below.

3. full of gloom _____

4. full of fun _____

Reading and Thinking

1. Check the sentence that tells the reason Charlie was scared in the story.

____ Charlie had never been in an airplane before.

____ Charlie had not flown solo before.

____ The airplane had not been checked.

2. Why do you think Charlie forgot there were other people in the universe?

_____

_____

List two facts that lead you to conclude that Charlie had a good first instructor.

3. _____

4. _____

Write the word that best completes each sentence.

5. The first pilots must have been very

_____ .

quiet   heroic   scary

6. Before Pat starts the engine, she does a

_____ check.

beginner's   altitude   preflight

Learning to Study

Many kinds of entry words can be found in most dictionaries. Match the types of entries with the correct examples.

1. ____ proper noun   **a. -ly**

2. ____ prefix   **b.** *learn the ropes*

3. ____ suffix   **c.** Ohio

4. ____ abbreviation   **d. mis-**

5. ____ idiom   **e.** Dr.

9

It's a Bird! It's a Plane!

Read to find out what the mystery is in this story.

1 "What is that?" Charlie screamed.

2 Pat almost jumped out of her seat as she shouted, "What is what?"

3 "It looks like a horrible prehistoric reptile," Charlie cried.

4 "Are you crazy? This is Washington, the District of Columbia. There aren't any prehistoric creatures here," Pat said.

5 To be sure, there were the familiar sights of Washington: the White House, the Washington Monument, the Lincoln Memorial, and the Capitol. Pat and Charlie certainly had not stepped back in time when they took off from National Airport.

6 "Maybe I'm seeing things too," Pat exclaimed as they turned to the north, "but is that it below us?"

7 "It sure is! I'd feel safer if we got out of here," Charlie said.

8 "Whew! Whatever it is sure looks real. Let's see if the control tower knows about it," Pat suggested.

9 Pat quickly switched on the radio and said, "Washington control, are we being invaded by a pterodactyl? There's an unbelievable creature down below that must have at least a fifteen-foot wingspread."

10 "It's not *a pair of duck tails*, Pat. It's a huge bird!" Charlie cried, trying to repeat what he had heard Pat say.

11 "Vista 5347 Victor, have you got a problem up there?" Frank, an air traffic controller, answered at last. "I know what you're looking at, but don't worry. It's not alive. It's a Smithsonian Institution model. The museum tested it out to see if an animal that big really could have flown. Its wings were powered by electric motors. The whole thing was controlled by a computer at the Smithsonian."

12 "Oh, now I remember," Pat said as Frank signed off. "It was modeled after the fossils they found in West Texas in the 1970s.

13 "Scientists believe it was the largest creature that ever flew," she continued. "The one we saw has an eighteen-foot wingspread, but the real ones were at least twice as big."

14 "Did it fly without a tail like this one?" Charlie asked.

15 "Yes," Pat explained, "supposedly it was able to move its wings back and forth to stay level and shift its weight to move through air currents."

16 "Well, it certainly looked real to me," Charlie said. "I thought for sure it was licking its chops when we flew over it."

17 "I was pretty startled myself," Pat added, "but I was trying to be reasonable. I figured that a sixty-five-million-year-old creature might have a little trouble catching us."

18 "You have nothing to worry about, Pat. The biggest birdbrains you have to deal with are those South American condors, whose wingspread is only nine feet, and me!" Charlie joked.

Knowing the Words

Write the words from the story that have the meanings below.

1. of the time before written history _____ (Par. 3)

2. extinct flying reptile _____ (Par. 9)

3. hardened animal or plant remains _____ (Par. 12)

4. large vultures _____ (Par. 18)

An **abbreviation** is a short form of a word or group of words. Write the words from the story that are represented by these abbreviations.

5. D.C. _____ (Par. 4)

6. n. _____ (Par. 6)

7. ft. _____ (Par. 9)

8. mus. _____ (Par. 11)

9. elec. _____ (Par. 11)

10. S.A. _____ (Par. 18)

Learning to Study

A **pronunciation key** is a list of sound symbols and key words that tell how to pronounce dictionary entry words. A pronunciation key can be found on the inside back cover of this book. Use this key to write the words that each of these respellings represents.

1. /hȯr´ ə bəl/ _____

2. /fə mil´ yər/ _____

3. /ter´ ə dak´ təl/ _____

4. /mod´ əl/ _____

5. /myü zē´ əm/ _____

Reading and Thinking

A **fact** is something that is known to be true. An **opinion** is what a person believes. An opinion may or may not be true. Write **F** for fact or **O** for opinion before each statement below.

1. ____ The hawk is a huge bird.

2. ____ The pterodactyl was scary.

3. ____ The Smithsonian Institution is in Washington, D.C.

4. ____ A condor's wingspread is nine feet.

Write **T** before statements that are true. Write **F** before those that are false.

5. ____ Pterodactyls were reptiles that are believed to have flown.

6. ____ The White House is in Washington, D.C.

7. ____ Pterodactyls are alive now.

8. ____ Pterodactyl fossils have not been found.

9. What did the Smithsonian do with the model? _____

_____

10. How did Pat know for sure they were flying over Washington, D.C.?

_____

Working with Words

The suffix **-able** or **-ible** means "capable of" or "tending to." Write the words from the story that have this suffix and that are formed from these base words.

1. horror _____ (Par. 3)

2. believe _____ (Par. 9)

3. reason _____ (Par. 17)

Nature's Own Aircraft

Read to find out how a bird is designed for flight.

1   Recently Pat's parents cleaned out their basement. They found a box of Pat's old school papers and sent them to her. Pat laughed when she saw a paper she had written after studying birds and reptiles when she was in the sixth grade. It was about how birds fly. The paper seemed especially interesting since she and Charlie had just seen a model of a pterodactyl. Here's what she had written.

2   **How Birds Fly**

   The prehistoric pterodactyl was a reptile that flew. Birds were most likely an early branch of the reptile group. Although birds and reptiles have many things in common, most birds, unlike most reptiles, have mastered the skill of flying. In fact, a bird's frame is designed for flight.

3   A bird's skeleton is light, yet remarkably strong. The bones are hollow and are braced by smaller bones. Other animals' bones are filled with tissue and usually are not braced.

4   The backbone of a bird, though short, is stronger and has fewer joints than that of most other animals. The skull is almost as thin as paper, which keeps the front part of the bird's body light for flying.

5   The bird's wings serve the same purpose as the engine and the wings of an airplane. The wings keep the bird in the air and move it through the air at the same time. Like other parts of a bird, the wings are strong and light. They are operated by sturdy muscles attached to the breastbone.

6   Not only are a bird's skeletal and muscular systems adapted for flight, but the feathers are also well constructed. They vary in size and weight according to their purpose. The biggest, stiffest feathers cover the wings.

7   Smaller feathers above and below the large feathers keep the air from passing

through. Because of this, a bird's wing can push against the air and get the most power out of each wing thrust.

8   In fact, the wing feathers overlap like shingles on a roof. The bird is able to move its feathers without loosening them, and therefore can control its flight. When a bird wants to slow down or land, it spreads the feathers at the tip of the wing farther apart. This creates a wider surface against which the air can push.

9   Tail feathers are also very important for a bird. A bird can spread its tail feathers and move them up and down to help in steering and stopping.

10   When a bird takes off, its wings move forward and backward, as well as up and down. To create this combined movement, a bird twists each wing as a unit. When a bird slows down to land, it spreads its wings and tail feathers and pushes them against the wind.

11   People have tried unsuccessfully to imitate a bird's capacity to fly. We have always dreamed about flying, but it is only in our dreams that our bodies are able to take off and fly like birds. The best we have been able to do is to build machines that are able to fly for us.

Knowing the Words

Write the words from the story that have the meanings below.

1. dealing with muscles _____ (Par. 6)

2. differ from _____ (Par. 6)

3. cover over _____ (Par. 8)

4. group acting as one _____ (Par. 10)

5. ability _____ (Par. 11)

In each row below, circle the two words that are related to the word in dark print.

6. **bird**   pterodactyl   condor   eagle
7. **airplane** fuselage   throttle   fossil
8. **people** dispatcher   terminal   parent
9. **skeleton** backbone   muscles   skull
10. **feathers**   skull   wing   tail

Working with Words

Possessives are words that show ownership. The singular possessive is usually formed by adding 's to a word. Rewrite each phrase below. Use possessive forms.

1. the wings of a bird

   _____

2. the body of an animal

   _____

3. the hat that belongs to Charlie

   _____

4. the message of the dispatcher

   _____

Write the compound words from the story that are formed by adding to these words.

5. back _____ (Par. 4)

6. lap _____ (Par. 8)

Reading and Thinking

1. Check the features that are common to birds as opposed to other animals.

   ____ They have paper-thin skulls.

   ____ Their bones are filled with tissue.

   ____ They have strong, short backbones.

   ____ They have wing and tail feathers.

2. Check the sentence that best expresses the main idea of this story.

   ____ Feathers help birds fly.

   ____ A bird is designed for flying.

   ____ Birds are different from reptiles.

3. Check the most likely conclusion you can make about Pat.

   ____ She was interested in flight in the sixth grade.

   ____ She knew a lot about reptiles.

   ____ She likes to save school papers.

Learning to Study

This graph shows the lengths of some birds. Under each bar on the graph, write the letter of the bird whose size is represented.

BIRD LENGTHS

a. swan—(1.5 meters)
b. hummingbird—(.15 meters)
c. ostrich—(2.43 meters)
d. eagle—(.76 meters)
e. hawk—(.46 meters)

2.43 m
2.13 m
1.83 m
1.50 m
1.22 m
.91 m
.61 m
.30 m
0 m

____ ____ ____ ____ ____

13

How Does an Airplane Fly?

Read to find out how a plane is able to get off the ground.

1   One Friday Pat was invited to a career day at her niece's middle school in South Bend. Pat was lucky enough to be able to arrange her flight schedule to be there. Her job was to talk to a class of sixth and seventh graders about what it was like to be a pilot. After giving a short speech, she asked for questions.

2   Surprisingly, the students didn't have any questions. They were all ears, though, when one of the teachers asked about flying. "Can you tell me how planes that weigh several tons are able to get off the ground?" Ms. Rynex asked.

3   "Well," Pat answered, "I had been flying for some time before I really understood it myself. All I knew was that if I drove down the runway fast enough and used the controls, the plane would lift. But the secret of flying is really simple. The trick is to weaken the pull of gravity on the aircraft.

4   "To understand how it can fly," Pat continued, "you need to know the parts of an airplane." As she spoke, Pat drew an airplane model on the chalkboard. "Like a bird, a plane has wings, or airfoils, and a body, or fuselage. It also has a tail assembly and landing gear. A plane is powered by jet engines or one or more engines that spin propellers. The engines and propellers can be in the front or back of the fuselage or in the wings.

5   "In order for a plane to fly, there are two sets of physical forces to counteract," Pat explained further. "It's sort of like two games of tug of war. On the end of one rope is *drag,* the force you feel pushing against you when you ride a bicycle. On the other end of that rope is *thrust.* Thrust is the force created by the plane's engines that moves the plane forward. To move forward, the thrust team must be stronger than the drag team.

6   "In the other game of tug of war, one end of the rope is *gravity,* the force that pulls things downward toward the earth. The other end of that rope is what we call *lift,* which does exactly what it says: it lifts the airplane off the ground.

7   "The wings of a plane are carefully designed to create lift. If you observe them, you'll notice that like bird wings, they are curved on top. When the plane moves forward, the air falls down the curved top of the wing. The air pressure below the wing tries to push it back up. Because the wing is in the way, this upward pressure lifts the wing instead.

8   "As the plane moves down the runway, the wing creates more lift. Finally the lift is greater than the force of gravity. Heavier planes must travel faster for a longer distance to create enough lift to enable them to get off the ground.

9   "Well," Pat concluded, "I think it all may sound more confusing than it really is. After being a pilot for several years, this knowledge has become second nature to me. Any more questions?"

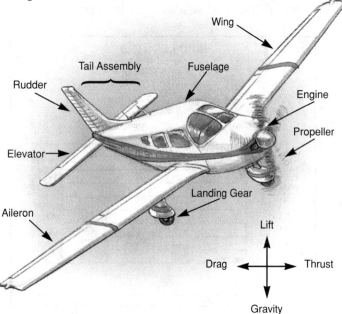

Knowing the Words

Write the words from the story that have the meanings below.

1. surfaces designed to lift a plane _____ (Par. 4)

2. devices with revolving blades used to move a boat or plane _____ (Par. 4)

3. go against _____ (Par. 5)

4. air pressure making a plane rise _____ (Par. 6)

5. allow _____ (Par. 8)

6. Check the sentence in which *drag* has the same meaning as in paragraph 5.

   ____ The minutes will drag until dinner.

   ____ The drag on the car forced the engine to work harder.

   ____ Can the horses drag the tractor out of the snowdrift?

7. Check the sentence in which *thrust* has the same meaning as in paragraph 5.

   ____ Spot thrust his way out the door.

   ____ I thrust the pin into the balloon.

   ____ The propeller created enough thrust to get the boat off the sandbar.

Working with Words

The suffix **-ward** means "in the direction of." Write the words from the story that have the suffix **-ward** and that are formed from these base words.

1. fore _____ (Par. 5)

2. down _____ (Par. 6)

3. to _____ (Par. 6)

4. up _____ (Par. 7)

Reading and Thinking

Write the word that best completes each sentence.

1. Gravity and drag are natural,

   _____ forces.

   adjoining   hazardous   physical

2. Air _____ creates lift.

   capacity   pressure   maneuver

3. The pilot increased engine power to

   create more _____.

   drag   gravity   thrust

Write **B** before statements that describe birds, write **P** before statements that describe planes, and write **B/P** before statements that describe both.

4. ____ They have curved wings.

5. ____ They have feathers.

6. ____ They have propellers.

7. ____ They have engines.

8. ____ They use lift and thrust to oppose gravity and drag.

Learning to Study

Different references provide different types of information. Write the name of the best reference to find each piece of information.

atlas   almanac   newspaper

dictionary   encyclopedia

1. how an airplane flies _____

2. definition of *airfoil* _____

3. map of Washington, D.C. _____

4. facts about airport sizes _____

5. weather forecast _____

15

Flying a Plane

Read to find out how a pilot controls a plane.

1 After Pat explained to her niece's classmates how a plane can get off the ground, they began asking questions. They wanted to know how to fly a plane.

2 "Is it like driving a car?" one girl asked.

3 "That's a good question," Pat said, "but I need to tell you a little more about planes to give you a good answer.

4 "Flying a plane is different from driving a car because a plane can move in more directions than a car can. When a plane turns left or right like a car, it's called a yaw. Moving the plane's rudder, the part of the plane that sticks up on the tail assembly, makes the plane yaw. Inside the cockpit, the pilot presses a left or right rudder foot pedal to turn the plane.

5 "Now, if a car were to dip to one side on two wheels, there would be the danger that it would roll over. But planes do this all the time in the air. It's called rolling or banking left or right. By raising or lowering the ailerons located on the back of a wing, the pilot can make the plane bank in one

direction or the other. Inside the cockpit, the pilot has a stick called a yoke that controls the ailerons.

6 "A car isn't made to take a nosedive or to take off into the air either," Pat continued. "But when a plane's nose makes this up and down movement, it's called a pitch. Moving the elevator, the part on the tail assembly that is level with the wings, causes the plane to pitch. The same yoke that controls the ailerons moves the elevator.

7 "The other control a pilot has is the throttle. Like a car's gas pedal, it controls the engine speed.

8 "On the ground, I have to steer my plane with my hands and feet. In order to turn left, for example, I have to push the left rudder pedal and move the yoke left and back at the same time."

9 "Why can't you just use one control?" someone asked.

10 "All the movements have to be controlled at the same time to keep the plane in balance. Using only one control would cause an airplane to skid. In a skid, the airplane is inefficient and may become uncontrollable," Pat answered.

11 "You really have to know a lot to be a pilot, don't you?" one boy asked.

12 "Yes!" Pat was quick to say. "You have to be able to handle the controls, read the instruments, and keep on course. You have to know about the weather, navigation, and flight regulations, too.

13 "I had over eighty hours of flight time before I got my private pilot's license," Pat explained. "I needed more training to become a commercial pilot."

14 Suddenly the bell rang, the students and teachers thanked Pat, and the school day was over. On their way home, Amy looked at her aunt and said, "Thanks a lot, Aunt Pat. You were so great," she giggled, "I think you deserve a *pat* on the back!"

Knowing the Words

Write the words from the story that have the meanings below.

1. side to side movement of the nose of a plane _____
   (Par. 4)

2. vertical flat piece on a plane's tail assembly causing yaw _____
   (Par. 4)

3. hinged parts on plane wings that make the plane roll _____
   (Par. 5)

4. lever that operates the elevators and ailerons _____
   (Par. 5)

5. part of a plane's tail assembly that causes pitch _____
   (Par. 6)

6. up and down movement of the nose of a plane _____
   (Par. 6)

Synonyms are words that have the same or nearly the same meanings. Write the words from the story that are synonyms for these words.

7. rolling _____
   (Par. 5)

8. pilot's stick _____
   (Par. 5)

9. laws _____
   (Par. 12)

Working with Words

The possessive of a plural word that ends in *s* is formed by adding an apostrophe after the *s*. For example, the plural possessive form of *friend* is *friends'*. Write a sentence that includes the plural possessive form of each word below.

1. plane _____

2. pilot _____

3. rudder _____

Reading and Thinking

1. What might happen if a pilot used only one control to make a maneuver?
   _____

2. Check the sentence that best expresses the main idea of this story.
   ——A pilot must know a lot.
   ——A plane has four basic controls.
   ——A plane has three basic movements.

3. A **summary** briefly gives facts about a topic. To summarize, you must find the most important facts and put them in an order that makes sense. In one sentence, summarize the information in paragraph 5.
   _____
   _____

Learning to Study

An **outline** is a form that shows how the important points in an article are related. Complete this partial outline for paragraphs 4 through 6 of this story.

I. Airplane Movements
   A. Yaw
      1. Plane Control: _____
      2. Pilot's Control: _____
   B. Roll or Bank
      1. Plane Control: _____
      2. Pilot's Control: _____
   C. Pitch
      1. Plane Control: _____
      2. Pilot's Control: _____

The Dream of Flight

Read to find out if people long ago thought about flying.

1   The week after Pat spoke at her niece's school, she and Charlie flew to the West Coast. As Charlie was checking the instruments during the flight, he thought about how close to the sun he was flying. Its light was so bright that the sun seemed near. Yet he knew it was about a hundred million miles away, and its temperature was a warm ten thousand degrees Fahrenheit.

2   At the same time, Pat was also daydreaming. "Do you think there was ever a time when people didn't think about flying?" she asked out of the blue. "I mean, I've wanted to fly all my life, but I knew it was possible. It was just a matter of getting the opportunity to do it. Maybe people don't think about something if they don't think it can be done."

3   "Oh, I'm sure people dreamed about flying and watched the birds to try to figure out how wings were different from arms," Charlie answered.

4   "How can you be sure?" asked Pat.

5   "Actually, I once read a Greek myth

about a man and his son who were able to fly. It had to have been written at least two thousand years ago," Charlie explained.

6   "I'm all ears," Pat said impatiently.

7   "Well," Charlie began, "in ancient Greece there was a man named Daedalus. He was a skillful architect. King Minos, the king of Crete, had Daedalus design and build a maze from which there was almost no escape. You could travel through it forever without finding the exit. To make things worse, inside the maze lived a cruel monster.

8   "King Minos learned that someone had killed this monster and that several prisoners had escaped. He knew Daedalus was the only one smart enough to have helped them. Daedalus had, in fact, told the girlfriend of one prisoner how to escape. He said that as the prisoner walked through the maze, he should leave a trail of string. If he wanted to escape, all he needed to do was to follow the string. As punishment for helping his enemies, King Minos imprisoned Daedalus and his son, Icarus, in the maze.

9   "But when Daedalus was sent into the maze, he did not have any string with him. He soon realized that the only way of escape was by air. For this purpose, he designed and made two pairs of wings.

10   "When the wings were complete, Daedalus warned Icarus not to fly too close to the sun. He told him that the beeswax adhesive that held the wings together might melt. Then father and son put on the wings and took off into the sky. But Icarus, being immature, was so thrilled with flying that he soared higher and higher, not paying any attention to his father's warning. When he neared the sun, the wings fell apart, and he dropped into the sea."

11   "What a sad story!" Pat exclaimed. "But you're right. People must have dreamed about flying to tell a story like that."

12   "But until the last two hundred years," Charlie said, "it was an impossible dream."

Knowing the Words

Write the words from the story that have the meanings below.

1. story or legend _____
   (Par. 5)

2. confusing
   network of paths _____
   (Par. 7)

3. put in jail _____
   (Par. 8)

4. substance that holds
   things together _____
   (Par. 10)

Write the actual meanings of these idioms.

5. *out of the blue* _____

6. *I'm all ears* _____

7. Check the sentence in which *figure* has the same meaning as in paragraph 3.

   ____ Divide this figure into that one to get the answer.

   ____ Did you figure out the mystery?

   ____ There was one lonely figure in the painting.

8. Check the sentence in which *right* has the same meaning as in paragraph 11.

   ____ Turn right at the corner.

   ____ The magazine was right there on the table.

   ____ You were right about the situation.

Working with Words

The prefix **im-** often means "not." Write the meaning of each word below.

1. impatient _____

2. immature _____

3. impossible _____

4. impolite _____

Reading and Thinking

1. Check the word that best describes the feeling or mood of the atmosphere in the cockpit.

   ____ scary   ____ humorous

   ____ relaxed   ____ tense

2. Check the word that best describes Minos.

   ____ ugly   ____ cruel

   ____ funny   ____ skillful

3. What do you think made Charlie think of the story about Daedalus and Icarus?

   _____

   _____

4. Check the conclusion you can make about the flying weather in this story.

   ____ The sky was dark and stormy.

   ____ The sky was full of snow.

   ____ There was a clear blue sky.

5. How hot is the sun?

   _____

Learning to Study

1. To find out more about Icarus, Daedalus, and King Minos, you could use reference sources. Put a **1** before the best source of this information. Put a **2** before the second-best source.

   ____ almanac   ____ encyclopedia

   ____ newspaper   ____ dictionary

   ____ atlas   ____ a book of myths

Write the names of two reference sources you could use to find facts about the sun.

2. _____

3. _____

An Impossible Dream

Read to find out how the Wright brothers achieved an impossible dream.

1 Pat had always been interested in history. She hadn't realized that her sixteen-year-old nephew, Bob, had the same interest until he wrote her this letter.

2 Dear Aunt Pat,

Mom said I should send you a report I wrote about the invention of the airplane. I'm usually not happy about writing papers, but this one was fun to do. Let me know what you think of it.

Bob

An Impossible Dream

3 At the turn of this century, two brothers put the dream of flight to the test. The men who successfully challenged the dream were Wilbur and Orville Wright.

4 The first steps toward flight had already been taken. Balloons and gliders had been afloat, but neither could be controlled. They floated and drifted at the mercy of the wind.

5 This new world of aeronautics captured the imagination of the Wrights. In 1900, in their bicycle repair shop, the brothers built a kite and then a two-winged glider. Using what they learned from these two aircraft, they set to work on an engine-powered biplane. They designed a craft with two wings, one above the other, like their glider.

6 For three years the brothers worked, building their own engine as well as the plane. At last their plane, the *Flyer*, was complete. It had a gasoline engine and wings made of wooden frames covered with cotton cloth. The *Flyer* was built so that the pilot could lie in the center of the bottom wing. To control the plane, a wire from each wing tip would be attached to the pilot's hips. By twisting the wings, the pilot could keep the plane balanced.

7 On December 17, 1903, at Kitty Hawk, North Carolina, Orville made a successful flight that covered 120 feet. In all, the brothers made four flights that day, taking turns. Minutes after the last flight, a gust of wind overturned the *Flyer* and damaged it. It never flew again.

8 Few people would acknowledge these historic flights. The Wrights then made more powerful planes and took them to Europe. When they received a number of awards in Europe, the United States finally took notice. People began to see the importance of the Wright brothers' achievements.

9 From the very start, the brothers had believed in a dream and in each other. Their work made an impossible dream come true and earned them a unique place in aviation history.

Knowing the Words

Write the words from the story that have the meanings below.

1. in the air _____
   (Par. 4)

2. science of flight _____
   (Par. 5)

3. aircraft with
   two sets of wings _____
   (Par. 5)

4. recognize _____
   (Par. 8)

5. special and unusual _____
   (Par. 9)

6. airplane flight _____
   (Par. 9)

An **antonym** is a word that is opposite in meaning from another word. Write the words from the story that are antonyms for these words.

7. sunk _____
   (Par. 4)

8. fixed _____
   (Par. 7)

9. gave _____
   (Par. 8)

10. failures _____
    (Par. 8)

Working with Words

The suffix **-ful** means "full of." Write the words from the story with the suffix **-ful** that are formed from these base words.

1. success _____
   (Par. 3)

2. power _____
   (Par. 8)

Write the words that have the suffix **-ful** and the meanings below.

3. full of grace _____

4. full of use _____

5. full of help _____

6. full of cheer _____

7. full of fear _____

Reading and Thinking

1. Check the conclusions you could make based on the fact that the Wright brothers took their airplane invention to Europe.

   _____ They thought they had an important invention.

   _____ They could speak French.

   _____ They were frustrated with the lack of recognition in the United States.

2. Why did the Wright brothers design a biplane rather than a plane with only one set of wings?

   _____

   _____

3. Number the events to show the order in which they happened.

   _____ The United States acknowledged the Wright brothers' achievement.

   _____ A gust of wind damaged the *Flyer.*

   _____ The brothers opened a bicycle shop.

   _____ The brothers built the *Flyer* and tested it at Kitty Hawk.

   _____ The brothers went to Europe.

   _____ The brothers built a glider.

Learning to Study

Refer to the pronunciation key on the inside back cover of this book to write the words that each of these respellings represents.

1. /ak nol´ ij/ _____

2. /ar´ ə nȯt iks/ _____

3. /ā´ lə ron´/ _____

4. /yu̇ nēk´/ _____

5. /yȯ/ _____

Ballooning

Read to find out how people were able to fly before engine-powered planes.

1   On the second weekend in May, Pat attended her ten-year college reunion. It was held in a small town in Massachusetts. Pat was happy to see friends whom she hadn't seen for a long time. She was disappointed that one person she had hoped to see wasn't there.

2   Twelve years ago she had met Ross, a young man who had come to Massachusetts from the South. He and Pat had a lot in common, and they really liked each other. Throughout the reunion weekend, she kept thinking about what fun they had had together. She remembered one special date when they saved some money, went to a county fair, and took a hot-air balloon ride.

3   Ross was able to tell Pat and the balloon pilot about the history of ballooning. He told them that the first balloon was built by two French brothers, the Montgolfiers. They had watched smoke rise from a fire. Then they were inspired to inflate a cloth bag with smoke to see if it would rise, too. They decided that smoke had some property that made things float.

4   Ross explained that in June, 1783, the brothers held a thirty-foot bag in the shape of a sphere over a smoking fire. The bag rose and traveled over a mile before the air inside cooled. Then the balloon landed.

5   Ross said that a few months after that flight, someone else used hydrogen to fill a silk balloon. The balloon rose and floated until it landed in a village fifteen miles away. When the people of the village saw the balloon descending, they thought it must be some kind of monster. The villagers grabbed their pitchforks and scythes and tore the balloon to bits.

6   Pat remembered that as Ross was telling this story, they had been flying over the New England countryside. The engine that produced the hot air that kept the balloon aloft started to make a weird sound. The balloon was fairly close to the ground when the engine quit. The balloon slowly descended into the middle of a cornfield.

7   When they were on the ground, Pat, Ross, and the pilot looked up to see some people running toward them. Instead of pitchforks, they had cameras. With the help of these people and the crew who had followed the balloon in a van, they packed the balloon. Then they headed back to the fairgrounds.

8   On the way back, Ross told them that the first balloon passengers had been a sheep, a rooster, and a duck. People didn't trust the effect high altitudes might have on themselves. The animals survived, and in November, 1783, people went into flight.

9   The week after their balloon ride, Ross and Pat had gone back to their homes for summer vacation. The next fall, Ross went to Georgia to study for a year. Although they wrote to each other, things weren't the same between them, and they drifted apart.

10   "Still," Pat thought to herself, "it would have been nice to see him."

Knowing the Words

Write the words from the story that have the meanings below.

1. blow up or swell
   with air or gas _____
   (Par. 3)

2. quality of something _____
   (Par. 3)

3. round figure _____
   (Par. 4)

4. colorless gas
   that burns easily _____
   (Par. 5)

5. Check the sentence in which *property* has the same meaning as in paragraph 3.

   ____ That book is my own property.

   ____ We own property in Utah.

   ____ Lemon juice has a sour property.

6. Check the sentence in which *rose* has the same meaning as in paragraph 5.

   ____ Ross gave Pat a yellow rose.

   ____ The smoke rose.

   ____ Your skirt is a rose color.

Working with Words

The prefix **in-** can mean "in, within, toward, into," or "on." Write the words from the story that have the prefix **in-** and come from these foreign base words.

1. *spirare*, meaning
   "to breathe" _____
   (Par. 3)

2. *flare*, meaning "blow" _____
   (Par. 3)

3. *sīd*, meaning "wide" _____
   (Par. 4)

Rewrite each phrase below. Use possessive forms.

4. the balloon of the Montgolfier brothers

   _____

5. the record for the world

   _____

Reading and Thinking

Write **T** before the statements that are true. Write **F** before those that are false.

1. ____ Hot-air balloons were flown before hydrogen balloons were flown.

2. ____ The first hot-air balloon was fifteen feet wide.

3. ____ The Montgolfiers used hydrogen to inflate the first balloon.

4. ____ Hot-air balloons are flown today.

5. ____ The Montgolfiers were English.

6. Why did the people of the village where the first hydrogen balloon landed tear the balloon to bits?

   _____

   _____

7. In one sentence, summarize the ballooning events of 1783.

   _____

   _____

   _____

Learning to Study

Guide words are the two words in dark print at the top of each page of a dictionary. These words are helpful in finding words quickly. Write the words from the list that would appear on a dictionary page that has each of the sets of guide words below.

   sphere   inflate   hydrogen   property

1. **helm—imprisoned** _____

2. **prehistoric—punctual** _____

3. **immature—inspired** _____

4. **spectacular—throttle** _____

Lighter Than Air

Read to find out what people have learned from balloon flight.

1   After Pat's first balloon ride, she was curious to know more about the history of balloon flights. She looked through newspapers, books, and magazines to find any information on balloons. She was fascinated by what she found.

2   She read about the 1978 flight of the *Double Eagle II*. It was the first helium balloon to make a transatlantic flight.

3   Two years later, one of the pilots from that flight and his son made the first nonstop balloon crossing of North America. Their balloon was the *Kitty Hawk.*

4   Then, in 1981, the *Double Eagle V* made the first crossing of the Pacific Ocean. Several years later, Joe W. Kittinger, Jr., made the first solo transatlantic flight. His balloon was the *Rosie O'Grady.*

5   Pat learned that in 1996 a young woman had set a new world's record for the longest time aloft in a hot-air balloon. The new record was fifteen hours and eleven minutes.

6   Pat also learned that it was in balloons that we discovered the effects high altitudes have on living things. She found out that a few years after the first balloon flights, two people made a balloon ascent. They found that at twenty-one thousand feet, they felt weak and their hearts were pounding. Their fingers were so numb that they had to pull the hydrogen release valve with their teeth to make a descent. The balloon descended to a level where oxygen revived them.

7   A few years later, a doctor found that it wasn't poisonous gases that caused this dazed condition at high altitudes. Instead, it was a lack of oxygen.

8   In 1875, three more scientists took a balloon trip to test the doctor's theory. They took bottles of oxygen with them. At twenty-one thousand feet, they noticed that their pulse rates had gone up. However, their brains signaled no alarm, and they weren't aware of the numbness of their hands.

9   One of the three opened a bottle of oxygen. In an instant, his awareness returned. He saw that the others were dead. Today we know that unconsciousness occurs at an altitude of twenty-five thousand feet. The dazed, senseless state is a sign that only thirty seconds of consciousness are left.

10   Pat also read about a woman named Dorothea Klumpke. Ms. Klumpke was the first woman to study the sky from a balloon. Pat realized that this was the first time people had been able to look at the sky from above the clouds. She also realized that balloons offered the first chance to watch the weather from above Earth's surface.

11   Pat learned a great deal about the usefulness of balloons after her first balloon ride. She found out that much of what we know about science is based on what balloonists discovered.

Photograph by Shafer & Hill / Tony Stone Images

Knowing the Words

Write the words from the story that have the meanings below.

1. colorless gas
that does not burn _____
(Par. 2)

2. crossing the
Atlantic Ocean _____
(Par. 2)

3. upward movement _____
(Par. 6)

4. unable to feel _____
(Par. 6)

5. part that
regulates flow _____
(Par. 6)

6. brought back to
consciousness _____
(Par. 6)

Write the words from the story that are **antonyms** (words that mean the opposite) of these words.

7. descent _____
(Par. 6)

8. alert _____
(Par. 7)

9. unconsciousness _____
(Par. 9)

Working with Words

The suffix **-ness** means "condition" or "quality." Write the words from the story that have the suffix **-ness** and the meanings below.

1. quality of being numb _____
(Par. 8)

2. quality of being aware _____
(Par. 9)

3. unconscious condition _____
(Par. 9)

4. useful quality _____
(Par. 11)

Choose two words with the suffix **-ness** from above and write a sentence for each.

5. _____

6. _____

Reading and Thinking

1. Write the word that best completes this sentence.

   The valve _____ hydrogen from the balloon.

   released   revived   imprisoned

2. Check the sentence that best expresses the main idea of this story.

   ____ Pat has learned a lot about balloons.

   ____ Ballooning helped people learn about oxygen.

   ____ Ballooning helped people learn a lot about the weather.

Write **F** for fact or **O** for opinion before each statement below.

3. ____ Dorothea Klumpke was the first woman to study the sky from a balloon.

4. ____ Early balloonists were brave.

5. ____ Hydrogen is lighter than air.

6. ____ Lack of oxygen causes unconsciousness.

7. Check the most likely reason the author had for writing this article.

   ____ to entertain

   ____ to inform

   ____ to persuade

Learning to Study

Complete this partial outline for the helium balloon records mentioned in the story.

Balloon Flight Records

I. First Transatlantic Flight

II. _____

III. _____

IV. _____

Early Giants of Flight

Read to find out why airships have almost disappeared.

1   At the end of May, Pat joined her sisters and their families for a picnic at her parents' home. The weather did not cooperate. The rain started in the morning and went on through the day. Most of the family stayed in the living room where Pat's father was recalling another rainy day.

2   "I was six years old and had just come in from playing in the rain with some friends," Mr. Berman said. "My parents had the radio on while they were making dinner. I knew something was wrong because the reporter sounded as if he were crying.

3   "It turned out," he added, "that fifty miles away in Lakehurst, New Jersey, a huge hydrogen dirigible, the *Hindenburg*, had burst into flames. Somehow the hydrogen had ignited during the landing. Over thirty people had been killed."

4   "Didn't that disaster bring an abrupt end to the building of airships?" asked Pat's sister, Lynda.

5   "Yes, for the most part," her mother explained. "Airships had so much promise, too. At one time, people were more excited about them than they were about airplanes. They provided the first commercial passenger and cargo service. They didn't move fast, but they could be steered through the air. This was a big advance over balloons that came before them."

6   "The first popular airships were those zeppelins named for the German count who built them," Mr. Berman added. "By the time the *Hindenburg* was destroyed, airships had become luxury liners. They had private rooms, dining rooms, and space for cargo."

7   "Why did they give up the whole project? Why didn't they change to a nonflammable gas like helium?" Lynda's son, Bob, asked.

8   "Well, there were a lot of other problems," his grandfather answered. "As your grandmother said, they didn't go very fast. Also, their great size was a disadvantage because huge hangars had to be built to house them. Airports had to be designed with special mooring masts for the airships. In fact, I think the tower of the Empire State Building in New York was meant to be a mooring mast, but no airship was ever able to dock there."

9   "Airships were so fragile that they faced the danger of wind and storm damage," Mrs. Berman added. "And besides, as Patty knows, airplanes were proving to be faster and more efficient."

10   "They're not all gone," Pat's niece, Amy, said. "I've seen a blimp before."

11   "Amy's right," her grandmother said. "Helium blimps are still used for advertising and as airborne platforms for TV cameras."

12   "Soup's on!" Pat's oldest sister Alice suddenly called as she walked in from the backyard. "This chicken may be a little wet, but it's properly grilled. Never let it be said that I let a little rain destroy a picnic."

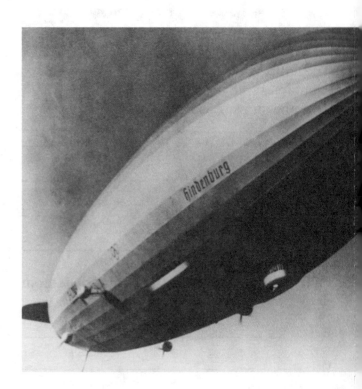

Photograph courtesy of Smithsonian Institution

Knowing the Words

Write the words from the story that have the meanings below.

1. airship _____
(Par. 3)

2. sudden _____
(Par. 4)

3. rigid airships named
for their inventor _____
(Par. 6)

4. places for anchoring _____
(Par. 8)

5. nonrigid airship _____
(Par. 10)

In each row below, circle the two words that are related to the word in dark print.

6. **airship**   blimp   fuselage   zeppelin

7. **hydrogen**   helium   oxygen   platform

8. Check the sentence in which *promise* has the same meaning as in paragraph 5.

_____ I promise to return your magazine.

_____ I will keep my promise.

_____ This student shows promise.

Working with Words

The prefix **dis-** means "not" or "opposite of." Write the words that have the prefix **dis-** and the meanings below.

1. not honest _____

2. not appeared _____

3. not an advantage _____

4. not approved _____

5. not courteous _____

Write the compound words from the story that are formed by adding to these words.

6. air _____
(Par. 6)

7. back _____
(Par. 12)

Reading and Thinking

Write the word that best completes each sentence.

1. The *Hindenburg* should have used a

_____ gas.

flammable   nonflammable   hydrogen

2. Airships needed huge _____.

hangars   zeppelins   dirigibles

3. The boat tried to _____ at the harbor.

burst   advance   dock

Write two of the reasons airships have almost disappeared.

4. _____

5. _____

6. Check the most likely conclusion you can make based on the fact that a nonflammable gas was used after the *Hindenburg* was destroyed.

_____ Airship travel grew.

_____ Airship travel was safer.

_____ Airship travel took more time.

_____ Airship travel was abandoned.

Learning to Study

The *Readers' Guide to Periodical Literature* is a book that contains a listing of a large number of magazine articles. The article subjects are arranged alphabetically. A new list comes out monthly. Below are four topics. Check the ones with which the *Readers' Guide* could be most helpful.

_____ the first balloon flight

_____ the *Hindenburg*

_____ the latest balloon flight record

_____ new developments in aviation

Soaring

Read to find out how gliders are different from airplanes.

1 "Are you ready?" Charlotte asked Pat.

2 The two friends were just about to take off on Pat's first ride in a glider. Charlotte signaled to Charlie in the tow plane ahead to prepare for takeoff.

3 "I'm nervous," Pat admitted. "I feel insecure without an engine."

4 "Just remember that gliders were around a long time before airplanes. In fact, I think the Wright brothers used what they learned from gliding to build the first airplane," Charlotte explained.

5 "Here goes nothing," Pat said as they started to move. She could see Charlotte's friend Mitchell running next to the right wing to keep the one-wheeled glider from tipping to one side.

6 When the plane was safely in the air, the towrope attached to the plane that had pulled the glider into the sky was released. Then Pat and Charlotte began soaring freely on the gentle wind.

7 "It's so quiet," Pat whispered, "I think I could hear a pin drop up here."

8 "That's what gives you the feeling of peace," explained her companion.

9 "That's if you believe you'll land in one *piece*," Pat laughed nervously.

10 "Very funny," Charlotte answered. "It's really not that different from flying a plane. The wings and fuselage are narrower than a plane's so that there is less drag, but the idea is the same. The biggest difference is that we have to be more aware of the air currents.

11 "Right now we're looking for an updraft to gain altitude," she continued. "See that hawk that is not flapping its wings? That's one indication of an updraft caused by wind hitting that hill and deflecting upward.

12 "We can also look for dark, dry, flat surfaces on the ground like roads and plowed fields," Charlotte added. "On a day like today, they absorb the sun's heat, and since hot air rises, it causes an updraft, too."

13 Pat was just beginning to relax when Charlotte said, "We could be in trouble."

14 "That's incredible!" Pat exclaimed. "We can't be out of fuel. There is no fuel!"

15 "I know, but there's no updraft here. We're not going to be able to return, so we have to make an immediate landing," Charlotte said without alarm.

16 The glider, or sailplane, was headed for a field of new grass. Pat gripped her seat, while Charlotte adjusted the wing flaps to control the angle of the downward glide. With a jolt, they were on the ground.

17 "See, Pat, we didn't fall to pieces, but we'll have to radio Mitchell to come get us. In the meantime, we'll dismantle the glider so we can load it onto the trailer."

18 By the time Mitchell arrived, the woman who owned the pasture had come out to see what had happened. Some cows were also investigating the situation.

19 "Well," Mitchell said, "that was a pretty exciting first flight for you, Pat."

20 "I couldn't forget this flight even if I wanted to," Pat laughed as she rubbed her bruised arm. "It was fun, but the landing made me sore from that soar!"

Knowing the Words

Write the words from the story that have the meanings below.

1. upward air movement _____ (Par. 11)

2. causing a change in direction _____ (Par. 11)

3. glider _____ (Par. 16)

4. take apart _____ (Par. 17)

A **pun** is a play on two words that sound alike or one word that has a double meaning. Pat used two puns in this story. Write the word that each pun refers to.

5. in one piece _____ (Par. 8)

6. made me sore _____ (Par. 20)

Write the words from the story that are synonyms (words that have the same or nearly the same meanings) for these words.

7. pull _____ (Par. 2)

8. jerk _____ (Par. 16)

9. field _____ (Par. 18)

10. examining _____ (Par. 18)

Working with Words

The prefix **in-** can mean "in, within, toward, into," or "on." It can also mean "not." Write the words from the story in which **in-** means "in" or "on" and that come from these foreign base words.

1. *dicare,* meaning "dedicate" _____ (Par. 11)

2. *vestigium,* meaning "footprint" or "track" _____ (Par. 18)

Write the words from the story in which **in-** means "not."

3. _____ (Par. 3.)   4. _____ (Par. 14)

Reading and Thinking

Write **G** before statements that describe gliders, write **A** before statements that describe airplanes, and write **G/A** before statements that describe both.

1. ____ They have wings and a fuselage.

2. ____ They are heavier than air.

3. ____ They use engines to propel them.

4. ____ They use updrafts to gain altitude.

5. ____ They have landing gear.

6. Check the word that best describes the weather in this story.

____ stormy   ____ foggy

____ sunny   ____ cloudy

7. Check the most likely story outcome.

____ Pat will never go soaring again.

____ Pat will take Charlotte on an adventurous airplane trip.

____ Pat will go soaring again.

8. Why do you think the sailplane was so quiet you could hear a pin drop?

_____

Learning to Study

The *Readers' Guide to Periodical Literature* is a book that contains a listing of magazine articles on many subjects. Use this sample listing to answer the questions below.

Soaring
The Wings of the Wind. J. Rubin. il. *Sport and Leisure* 132:117-24, O 14 '87.

1. What is the subject? _____

2. What is the title of the article?

_____

3. What is the date it was published?

_____

Unfinished Story

Read to find out about the mystery that was never solved.

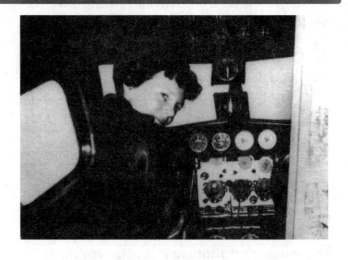

1   History is full of unfinished stories, unanswered questions, and unsolved mysteries. When she was in the sixth grade, Pat read about one of history's unsolved mysteries when she read a biography of Amelia Earhart. Earhart became one of the people Pat most admired because of her spirit. But Pat was always intrigued by what happened to her.

2   Amelia Earhart would have been an extraordinary person in any time and place. The United States in the 1920s and 30s, though, was a perfect setting for her. Flying was a risky business then. It was filled with challenge, danger, and thrills, and it drew her like a magnet.

3   Born in Atchison, Kansas, in 1898, Earhart worked as a nurse during World War I. Then she was a social worker before she went to California to earn money for flying lessons.

4   Breaking into the world of aviation wasn't easy. There were very few women in aviation in the 1920s. It was a while before she was accepted, but she had a lot going for her. Her flying skills were excellent, she was willing to work hard, and she was calm under pressure. She was also a warm, friendly person.

5   Fame came to Earhart suddenly in June 1928. As a passenger, she was the first woman to cross the Atlantic Ocean in an airplane. Overnight she was one of the most famous women in the world. Since she had been just a passenger on the flight, she did not feel she deserved the recognition.

6   She logged more flying hours after that. She wanted to gain more experience. Then she could set some flight records of which she could be proud. After she married publisher George Putnam, she became the first woman to fly alone across the Atlantic in May 1932. Then, she flew nonstop across the United States. This flight set a new women's record. Next, she was the first person to fly solo across the Pacific Ocean.

7   In 1937 she took on flying's greatest challenge. She and navigator Fred Noonan would try to fly around the world. They left Florida on May 21 and flew eastward.

8   They flew more than two thirds of the way. Then they had to fly across the Pacific from New Guinea. Their goal was to reach Howland Island, but they never did. On July 2, 1937, less than a month before her thirty-ninth birthday, Earhart's plane disappeared without a trace. Nothing was ever found, in spite of one of the most extensive searches in history.

9   Two years later, Earhart's husband wrote *Soaring Wings*. That was the biography that Pat later read. But to this day, no one knows for sure what happened to Amelia Earhart. Some people speculate that the plane had engine trouble and crashed into the sea. Others believe that it ran out of fuel. Some even think the crew may have been captured by the Japanese. There are those who don't accept any of these answers. They want to continue to look for another solution. Like a puzzle with a missing piece, the story of Amelia Earhart remains a mystery.

Photograph courtesy of Smithsonian Institution

Knowing the Words

Write the words from the story that have the meanings below.

1. fascinated _____
   (Par. 1)

2. special notice _____
   (Par. 5)

3. bit of evidence _____
   (Par. 8)

4. far reaching _____
   (Par. 8)

5. guess _____
   (Par. 9)

Write the words from the story that are represented by these abbreviations.

6. U.S. _____
   (Par. 2)

7. KS _____
   (Par. 3)

8. CA _____
   (Par. 3)

9. Atl. _____
   (Par. 5)

10. Pac. _____
    (Par. 6)

11. FL _____
    (Par. 7)

12. Is. _____
    (Par. 8)

Learning to Study

Below is a map showing the area where Earhart's plane vanished. Look at the map and then fill in the information.

1. Starting point _____

2. Intended destination _____

3. Direction headed _____

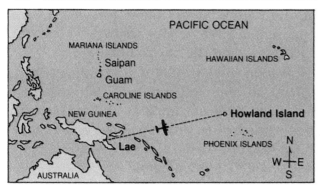

Reading and Thinking

1. Number the events to show the order in which they happened to Earhart.

   _____ She flew solo across the Atlantic.

   _____ She tried to fly around the world.

   _____ She worked as a nurse.

   _____ George Putnam wrote her story.

   _____ She became the first woman to cross the Atlantic.

   _____ She vanished with no trace.

2. Check the sentence that best expresses the main idea of this story.

   _____ Fame came to Earhart in 1928.

   _____ Earhart was a remarkable person.

   _____ Earhart was the first woman to fly solo across the Atlantic.

Write **F** for fact or **O** for opinion before each statement below.

3. _____ Earhart's flying skills were excellent.

4. _____ Earhart married a publisher.

5. _____ Earhart became the first woman to fly across the Atlantic Ocean.

6. _____ Amelia Earhart was the greatest pilot.

Working with Words

Write the compound words from the story that are formed by adding to these words.

1. ordinary _____
   (Par. 2)

2. night _____
   (Par. 5)

Write the words from the story that contain the suffixes below.

3. -y _____
   (Par. 2)

4. -ly _____
   (Par. 4)

One of a Kind

Read to find out about this famous pilot.

1 Another person Pat admires is Charles Lindbergh. To Pat, his colorful life seemed filled with adventure. It spanned almost the whole history of aviation. He was one year old when the Wright brothers made their first flight. As he grew up on a farm in Minnesota, he had no idea that he would be one of the most famous pilots of all time.

2 What he did know was that he was fascinated with mechanical things. He knew also that he had a talent for making things run. In 1922, he enrolled in a flying school without ever having flown in a plane. He was that convinced he wanted to fly. After just a few lessons, it was clear that he was a born pilot.

3 It was his dream to have his own plane. To make money, he sometimes worked as a mechanic's helper. Other times he did daredevil stunts to attract crowds who might later pay for a plane ride.

4 In 1924, Charles Lindbergh entered the Army Air Service, where he finished at the top of his class. After graduation, he went to St. Louis, Missouri. He worked there as a mail pilot. There he saw a chance to try for a $25,000 prize. It was for the first solo, nonstop crossing of the Atlantic by air. For over eight years no one had claimed the prize. Charles Lindbergh convinced some St. Louis business people to pay his flight expenses. These expenses included the cost of the plane, which he named *Spirit of St. Louis.*

5 First, he tested the plane on a record-setting transcontinental flight. Then on May 20, 1927, he left New York. He landed near Paris, France, 3,600 miles and thirty-three and a half hours later.

6 After that, his life was never the same. He was nicknamed *Lone Eagle* and *Lucky Lindy.* His reputation had become larger than life. But being in the public eye was hard for him. He needed privacy.

7 Two years after the flight, he married Anne Morrow and taught her to fly. Together they made several expeditions charting courses for future airline routes. She later became famous in her own right for her poems and books.

8 Tragedy struck in 1932. The Lindberghs' young son was kidnapped and later found dead. To escape the publicity, the Lindberghs moved to Europe for a few years.

9 Though he is remembered as a pilot, Charles Lindbergh was a man of many talents. He wrote books about his life and worked as an adviser for the airlines. He also served as an adviser to the U.S. government. When he was older, he spoke out for nature conservation. In fact, he opposed supersonic jets because he feared their effects on the environment.

10 Pat saw a picture of him standing with the crowd that watched *Apollo 8* blast off for the moon. She was impressed that this man had witnessed so much of flight history. When he died in 1974, aviation lost one of its most gifted champions.

Knowing the Words

Write the words from the story that have the meanings below.

1. entered _____
   (Par. 2)

2. crossing of
   a continent _____
   (Par. 5)

3. terrible situation _____
   (Par. 8)

4. public recognition _____
   (Par. 8)

5. natural surroundings _____
   (Par. 9)

Write the phrases from the story that are idioms and have these meanings.

6. exaggerated _____
   (Par. 6)

7. being famous _____
   (Par. 6)

8. through her own efforts

   _____
   (Par. 7)

Write the words from the story that are synonyms (words that have the same or nearly the same meanings) for these words.

9. alone _____
   (Par. 4)

10. trips _____
    (Par. 7)

Working with Words

The suffix **-er** can mean "identity of." Write the words from the story that have the suffix **-er** and the meanings below.

1. one who helps _____
   (Par. 3)

2. one who advises _____
   (Par. 9)

The suffix **-er** can also mean "more." Write the words from the story that have **-er** and the meanings below.

3. more large _____
   (Par. 6)

4. more old _____
   (Par. 9)

Reading and Thinking

Write **T** before sentences that are true.
Write **F** before those that are false.

1. _____ Charles Lindbergh made the first nonstop, solo, transatlantic flight.

2. _____ Charles Lindbergh knew the Wright brothers.

3. _____ Charles Lindbergh had not flown before winning the $25,000 prize.

4. _____ Anne Lindbergh was an author.

5. Check the words that describe Charles Lindbergh.

   _____ daring   _____ mysterious

   _____ cruel   _____ skillful

   _____ shy   _____ fearful

6. Why hadn't a nonstop, transatlantic flight been made before 1927?

   _____

   _____

Learning to Study

A time line shows the order of events. Use this time line of part of Charles Lindbergh's life to answer the questions below.

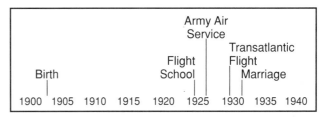

1. What amount of time is represented in

   this time line? _____

2. Read the events below. Then check those furthest apart in the time line.

   _____ Flight School and Marriage

   _____ Birth and Flight School

   _____ Army Air Service and Marriage

The Best

Read to find out about different aviation records.

1 Pat was asked by a local paper to write a short story about airplane flight records and some of the pilots who made them. This is what she wrote.

2 **The Best**

Apart from Charles Lindbergh's and Amelia Earhart's notable flights, many think that the biggest achievement in aviation was a trip around the world. The first of these was made in 1924. The journey took one hundred seventy-five days, and the plane's crew landed in twenty-nine countries. When the flight was over, one pilot said, "We wouldn't do it again for a million dollars!"

3 Others did try to make this trip. The first woman to fly solo around the world was Jerrie Mock. In 1964, her trip took thirty days.

4 The record for the fastest flight around the world is held by Brooke Knapp. In 1984, she flew 23,359 miles in forty-five and one-half hours.

5 The record for nonstop flight around the world without refueling was the "last plum in aviation records." These were the words of pilot Dick Rutan. On December 14, 1986, he and Jeana Yeager took off from California in the *Voyager*. Nine days and three minutes later, they landed in the same spot after traveling 25,012 miles in a cabin that seemed smaller than a bathtub.

6 More records have been made and broken, too. The first man to break the sound barrier was Chuck Yeager, who is not related to Jeana Yeager. In 1947, he flew 967 miles per hour. The first woman to pass the sonic barrier was Jacqueline Cochran in 1953.

7 The most recent record for flight speed was made in 1976. The fastest speed so far flown is 2,193.17 miles per hour. The record for plane altitude was set the next year. It stands at 123,523.58 feet.

8 The record for the lowest flight is held by Kathleen Snaper. In 1979, she flew below sea level for more than four hours in California's Death Valley.

9 The longest anyone has stayed aloft is sixty-four days and twenty-two hours. This record was set in 1958.

10 The smallest plane was first flown in 1984. It was just over nine feet long and had a six-foot wingspread. The largest planes belong to the U.S. Air Force. They are more than 250 feet long.

11 In 1987, Lois McCallin set the women's record for human-powered flight. She pedaled ten miles in just over thirty-seven minutes. The next day, Glen Tremml broke the men's record. In his pedal-driven plane, he flew about thirty-seven miles over the Mohave Desert. The flight lasted two hours and fourteen minutes.

12 The next feat of foot power was a flight from Crete to Greece. A plane named *Daedalus* was designed to make this trip. With the *Daedalus*, the dream of flight came full circle. It started with the mythical Daedalus and his wings of wax and feathers. But this time, there wasn't any danger of flying too close to the sun.

Knowing the Words

Write the words from the story that have the meanings below.

1. outstanding _____
   (Par. 2)

2. something that
   blocks the way _____
   (Par. 6)

3. relating to sound _____
   (Par. 6)

4. daring accomplishment _____
   (Par. 12)

Hyperbole is a figure of speech in which exaggeration is used to make a point. For example, if something were heavy, someone might say, "It weighs a ton!" On the first line below, write the phrase in the story that is an example of hyperbole. Underneath, write the true meaning of each phrase.

5. _____
   (Par. 2)

   _____

6. _____
   (Par. 5)

   _____

Working with Words

Rewrite each phrase below. Use possessive forms.

1. the notable flights of Amelia Earhart

   _____

2. the voyage of the *Daedalus*

   _____

3. the Mohave Desert of California

   _____

4. the records of aviators

   _____

5. the flight of Chuck Yeager

   _____

Reading and Thinking

1. What can you conclude based on the fact that Rutan and Yeager flew a longer distance around the world than Brooke Knapp did?

   _____

   _____

2. Check the phrase that best expresses the main idea of Pat's article.

   ____ Flight Records

   ____ Famous Aviators

   ____ The Dream of Flight

3. Check the most likely prediction you can make based on the information in this story.

   ____ More records will be broken.

   ____ No more records will be made.

   ____ Existing records won't be broken.

4. In one sentence, summarize paragraph 5.

   _____

   _____

Learning to Study

Complete this partial outline for the article you just read. The first one is done for you.

I. Round-the-World Flight Records

    A. 1924 First Flight _____

    B. _____

    C. _____

    D. _____

II. Sonic Barrier Records

    A. _____

    B. _____

Like Birds in Flight

Read to find out how Pat feels about flying in an ultralight.

1   On one particular sunny day, Pat's adventurous friend, Charlotte, finally convinced her to fly in an ultralight. Charlotte's friend Juan agreed to train her.

2   "I'm surprised you haven't tried this already, Pat," Juan said. "A lot of airline pilots fly these gliders all the time."

3   "Well, give me a chance," Pat said. "Ultralights haven't been around for too long, have they?"

4   "Well, the idea started with the Wright brothers," Juan explained. "It just got off track. It wasn't until 1975 that the ultralight was born, when a man named John Moody attached a ten-horsepower engine and a propeller to a hang glider and took off.

5   "Now there are thousands of ultralights in the air. I made this one," Juan continued as he made his preflight check, "out of a kit that I bought for nine thousand dollars.

6   "The first ultralights were controlled by shifting the pilot's weight," Juan said, "but this one has a yoke and throttle control. It climbs to over ten thousand feet and goes up to fifty-five miles per hour. It weighs only about two hundred and fifty pounds. This one has two seats because I use it for training. Isn't it beautiful?" he boasted.

7   "What Pat really wants to know, Juan," Charlotte interrupted, "is if it's safe."

8   "Well, I can't say that some people haven't been hurt," Juan admitted, "but the accident rate is lower than that of other aircraft. You see, the ultralight doesn't travel very fast, it lands slowly and gently, and it carries less than five gallons of fuel. These circumstances prevent a blow-up type of crash."

9   Juan and Pat put on their helmets and buckled themselves into the seats.

Charlotte, who was staying on the ground, could see that Pat was anxious.

10   Juan started the motor. "Honestly, you have nothing to worry about, Pat. Just relax and enjoy the ride!"

11   "I will, I will," Pat laughed nervously.

12   With that, the little glider sprang to life and began moving down the pavement. Before Pat knew it, she and Juan were airborne. The faithful engine was pushing them higher and higher into the sky.

13   Pat had never experienced anything like this. She felt like a bird in flight. She held out her arms and felt the warm air. She looked up at the smiling sun and down at the earth. All her fears were forgotten.

14   Suddenly a hawk appeared from nowhere. It flew directly in front of the ultralight, taunting the humans inside. The hawk banked to the left, and Juan did the same. Then it banked to the right, and the ultralight followed. Then as suddenly as it had appeared, it dived underneath the glider, disappeared, and laughed as if to say, "There are still some things you can't do!"

15   Back on the ground, Pat made plans with Juan to meet again. "I can hardly wait," Pat said. "That was really flying!"

Knowing the Words

Write the words from the story that have the meanings below.

1. separate or special _____
(Par. 1)

2. engine-powered
   hang glider   _____
(Par. 1)

3. measure of
   engine power _____
(Par. 4)

4. conditions _____
(Par. 8)

5. teasing _____
(Par. 14)

Personification is a figure of speech in which an author writes about an idea or thing as if it had lifelike or human qualities. For example, in paragraph 12, the glider was personified when it "sprang to life" because a glider cannot be alive. Write the words or phrases that show how these objects or animals are personified in this story.

6. engine _____
(Par. 12)

7. sun _____
(Par. 13)

8. hawk _____
(Par. 14)

Working with Words

The prefix **ad-** means "to" or "toward." Write the words from the list that come from these foreign base words.

admit   adjoining   adhesive   advance

1. *ante*, meaning
   "before"   _____

2. *mittere*, meaning
   "to send"   _____

3. *haerere*, meaning
   "to stick"   _____

4. *jungere*, meaning
   "to join"   _____

Reading and Thinking

1. Check the statement that best describes Pat in this story.

   ____ She will not try new things.

   ____ She loves to try new things.

   ____ She will try something new once, but will not try it again.

   ____ She may be afraid, but she will try new things anyway.

2. Why can't you find the word *ultralight* in an older dictionary?

   _____

   _____

Write **T** before statements that are true.
Write **F** before those that are false.

3. ____ Ultralights weigh less than hang gliders.

4. ____ Ultralights have small engines.

5. ____ Some ultralights can fly as high as ten thousand feet.

6. ____ Ultralights can travel at supersonic speeds.

7. Check the facts below that contribute to the safety of ultralights.

   ____ They don't travel very fast.

   ____ They are reasonably inexpensive.

   ____ They land slowly and gently.

   ____ They were invented recently.

   ____ They don't carry much fuel.

Learning to Study

An encyclopedia has a lot of information. Check the subjects you could look up in an encyclopedia to learn about ultralights.

____ Aviation   ____ Aircraft

____ World War II ____ Kitty Hawk

Workhorse of the Sky

As you read, look for differences between helicopters and other types of aircraft.

1   At a recent staff meeting, Howard, the cargo manager, introduced Pat and Charlie to Kim Harris. Kim had just been hired by their company to fly a cargo helicopter.

2   Kim explained to Pat that during the past fifteen years she had held a lot of different jobs. For three years she had been a pilot for a traffic news service. Then she transferred to an air taxi company. While there she transported up to thirty commuters from place to place each day.

3   When she had been with the taxi service for a year, she was offered a job with an agricultural air service out West. There she was called to herd cattle by air. She also sprayed crops with fertilizer. While working for this service, she was sent to Washington one spring when a killing frost was expected. She spent one night flying over an apple orchard to force warm air down on the budding trees.

4   She was well paid at the agricultural service, but she missed her friends and family in the Midwest. As soon as she could, she moved to the Great Lakes region. There she got a job flying an enormous helicopter. This chopper towed ships to port, loaded and unloaded freight, and carried cargo to construction sites.

5   One day, she heard that an emergency flight service needed chopper pilots. She called to ask about the job and was hired the next week. She was on call to fight fires, to get helpless people out of remote places, and to supply aid to disaster areas.

6   "Now that took nerve!" Kim exclaimed. "I often had to design my own heliport. In some places, it was hard to find a flat piece of land bigger than a postage stamp!"

7   A helicopter is an extraordinary craft. Unlike an airplane, it doesn't require a runway. Instead, it lifts straight up to take off and comes straight down to land as if it were weightless. It can move forward, backward, or sideways in the air. It can even remain motionless or stay in one spot and turn all the way around.

8   Helicopters have been around more than fifty years. It was only after the Second World War that a practical design was built. All of the models before that were too awkward and couldn't be controlled.

9   Helicopters fly by means of a large rotor or airfoil and a much smaller tail rotor. The large rotor is right above the cockpit. It spreads parallel to the ground and rotates to the left. The smaller tail rotor faces out to the side and spins to the right. Since the two rotors spin in opposite directions, the helicopter doesn't whirl out of control.

10   Kim told Pat that she finally felt she had found a job where she could stay for a long time. "I'm near my family, and this eggbeater is fairly safe," she explained. "I really do like what I do, and so far I like the people here, too!"

Knowing the Words

Write the words from the story that have the meanings below.

1. people who travel back
   and forth from work _____
   (Par. 2)

2. courage _____
   (Par. 6)

3. airport designed
   for helicopters _____
   (Par. 6)

4. spinning airfoil _____
   (Par. 9)

Write the words from the story that are synonyms (words that have the same or nearly the same meanings) for these words.

5. distant _____
   (Par. 5)

6. remarkable _____
   (Par. 7)

7. useful _____
   (Par. 8)

8. spins _____
   (Par. 9)

Write the two synonyms that are used in the story for the word *helicopter.*

9. _____
   (Par. 5)

10. _____
    (Par. 10)

Working with Words

The suffix **-less** means "without" or "not having." Write the words with the suffix **-less** that are formed from these base words.

1. help _____

2. weight _____

3. motion _____

Write the meaning of each word below.

4. effortless _____

5. doubtless _____

6. childless _____

Reading and Thinking

Write two things about helicopters that make them practical.

1. _____

2. _____

3. Why don't the two rotors of the helicopter turn in the same direction?

   _____

Write **H** before statements that describe a helicopter, and write **A** before statements that describe an airplane.

4. ____ requires a runway

5. ____ has wings

6. ____ can stay in one spot in the air

7. ____ can move straight up and down

8. Check the most likely conclusion about helicopters you can make.

   ____ They are easy to repair.

   ____ They are unique among aircraft.

   ____ They are not practical.

Learning to Study

Dictionary entry words are often divided into syllables. This shows where the words should be divided at the end of a line of writing. Write the words below, and leave spaces between the syllables.

1. helicopter _____

2. directions _____

3. A **thesaurus** is a type of dictionary in which synonyms are grouped. Check the words you might look up in a thesaurus to find synonyms for *helicopter.*

   ____ aircraft   ____ airport

   ____ helicopter   ____ aviator

Future Planes

Read to see what kinds of changes may take place in air travel in the future.

1   Pat and Geoff, another Vista pilot, were watching a team of mechanics complete a routine maintenance check on the Vista. All of them were talking about the new car models that had just come out. Then Geoff said, "Hey, Carol, you read science fiction. What will the planes of the future be like?"

2   Carol continued to work on the plane as she answered, "You don't have to read science fiction to find out. The aviation industry is already giving us some clues about what the future will be like."

3   "What do you mean?" Pat asked.

4   "Well," answered Carol, "we already have a supersonic jet that can fly at 1,350 miles per hour, or about twice the speed of sound. It's just a matter of time before these aircraft will be commonplace."

5   "Wow! It probably doesn't get any faster than that, does it?" Geoff asked.

6   "For right now, it is the fastest passenger jet. But there are companies hoping to develop transports that can fly at three times the speed of sound. However, there are environmental problems to iron out first," Carol replied.

7   "Just think," Pat said, "if I flew a supersonic jet, I could get to Europe in less than four hours. Right now, it takes over seven hours in most passenger jets."

8   "You know, speed is not the only change for planes of the future," Carol went on.

9   "What else could there possibly be?" Geoff wondered.

10   "Airliners that can take off with little or no runway," answered Carol. "They would fly at more than three hundred miles per hour. And they would carry about two hundred people. With more people traveling by air and less space for runways, these aircraft would be very practical.

11   "Another solution for the problems of overcrowded airports and delays caused by so many people flying," Carol continued, "might be bigger jets. Right now the biggest jets can carry about five hundred and sixty-six passengers. But some companies are designing jets that can carry eight hundred people! Who knows, maybe they'll even have stores and restaurants in them.

12   "And with the space shuttle already in regular use, maybe someday passengers will be making round trips to the moon," Carol added with a gleam in her eye.

13   Pat said, "Now that sounds like science fiction! That won't happen in our lifetime."

14   "You never know," Carol remarked. "It's been less than a hundred years since the first plane. Aviation has gone far beyond the wildest dreams of the early aviators."

15   "That's true," said Geoff. "It's likely much more than we can dream will be possible."

Photograph by H. Armstrong Roberts, Inc.

Knowing the Words

Write the words from the story that have the meanings below.

1. upkeep _____
   (Par. 1)

2. faster than the
   speed of sound _____
   (Par. 4)

3. ordinary _____
   (Par. 4)

4. having to do with
   your surroundings _____
   (Par. 6)

5. answer _____
   (Par. 11)

6. space vehicle _____
   (Par. 12)

7. Check the sentence in which *iron* has the same meaning as in paragraph 6.

   _____ Take the iron out of the box.

   _____ Tom needs to iron out the bugs in his invention.

   _____ You should iron that shirt.

In each row below, circle the two words that are related.

8. transports   problems   airliners

9. delay   speed   supersonic

Working with Words

The suffix **-al** means "relating to." Write the words from the story that have the suffix **-al** and that are formed from these base words.

1. environment _____
   (Par. 6)

2. practice _____
   (Par. 10)

Write the words that have the suffix **-al** and the meanings below.

3. relating to economy _____

4. relating to fiction _____

5. relating to politics _____

Reading and Thinking

Write the word that best completes each sentence.

1. Large numbers of people flying can

   cause _____ airports.

   complete   overcrowded   practical

2. Careful thought is needed to find

   _____ to problems.

   passengers   delays   solutions

3. Check the sentence that best expresses the main idea of this story.

   _____ The aviation industry is giving clues about the future of aviation.

   _____ Some planes can travel more than two times the speed of sound.

   _____ Early aviators did not dream their planes would lead to the aircraft of today.

4. Check the most likely reason the author had for writing this story.

   _____ to entertain

   _____ to inform

   _____ to persuade

Learning to Study

The signs below are currently used to help travelers locate necessary services. Match the signs with the services below.

1. _____ ticket purchases   a. 🚗

2. _____ car rental   b. 🧳

3. _____ restaurant   c. ✈

4. _____ information   d. 🚹

5. _____ air transportation   e. ?

6. _____ baggage   f. 🍴

41

High Fliers

Keep a count of the different kinds of kites that are mentioned in this story.

1   "Go fly a kite!" Pat had told Charlie after one of his ridiculous stories.

2   "This weekend," Charlie had responded, "that's just what I plan to do." The city was sponsoring its annual kite festival. Charlie had made an old-fashioned box kite to fly.

3   On the way to the festival, he thought about the vacation he had taken in Asia two years before. It was there he learned that the first kites had been flown in China over three thousand years ago. On his trip he got to see a Chinese dragon kite. It was constructed of a series of bamboo circles covered with paper. Each circle was connected by cords to the next. In the wind the dragon kite wriggled like a giant snake.

4   In Japan, he saw the largest kite he had ever seen. The kite was almost eight hundred square feet and weighed more than five hundred pounds. It took two hundred people to carry the kite to a plateau between two mountain ranges. When the enormous kite lifted off, some people at the ropes were lifted off their feet by it.

5   Charlie learned that in the sixteenth century, explorers coming back from Asia brought kites to Europe. In Asia kites had been used in ceremonies. In Europe they were used for scientific experiments and as toys. This was before the time of balloons and other aircraft.

6   This day Charlie and the other kite enthusiasts were out for pure fun. As he drove to the big field, he could see that the show had begun.

7   In the brilliant blue sky, he could see diamond-shaped flat and bowed kites with their colorful tail ribbons. There were also several box kites and one or two triangular kites. There was even a flexible kite that looked like an enormous parachute.

8   Within seconds, Charlie was out on the field, and, surprisingly, there was Pat looking for him. "It's such a perfect day for kite flying," she said, "that I just couldn't miss the show."

9   "It certainly is perfect," Charlie agreed. "These ten-mile-an-hour winds are not too strong and not too light. Will you give me a hand at launching my kite?"

10   "Sure," Pat said as he handed her the kite. She turned and walked about fifty-five feet against the wind and then released the kite. Immediately it rose into the sky. By tightening the line, Charlie urged it higher, where the breezes were steadier.

11   People flew their kites for several hours. Then the prizes for the best kites were awarded. A woman who had been making and flying kites for over fifty years had won a prize for the best design. A twelve-year-old girl had won one for endurance. Charlie hadn't won any prizes, but he had had a great day.

12   "You know," said Pat as they headed for home, "when I told you to go fly a kite yesterday, I didn't mean for you to take me seriously, but I'm glad you did."

Knowing the Words

Write the words from the story that have the meanings below.

1. supporting _____
   (Par. 2)

2. interested people _____
   (Par. 6)

3. sending up or out _____
   (Par. 9)

4. ability to last _____
   (Par. 11)

In each row below, circle the two words that are related.

5. enormous   huge   ridiculous

6. flexible   triangular   bowed

Find and write the idioms in the story that are figurative ways of saying these phrases.

7. "leave me alone"

   _____
   (Par. 1)

8. "help me" _____
   (Par. 9)

9. Check the sentence in which *mean* has the same meaning as in paragraph 12.

   ____ Did you mean what you said?

   ____ That dog is not really mean.

   ____ That woman flies a mean kite.

Working with Words

Hyphenated compound words are formed by putting two or more words together with hyphens to make a new word. Write the hyphenated compound words from the story that are formed by adding a word or words to each word below.

1. old _____
   (Par. 2)

2. diamond _____
   (Par. 7)

3. five _____
   (Par. 10)

4. year _____
   (Par. 11)

Reading and Thinking

1. Check the word that best describes the mood of this story.

   ____ scary   ____ humorous

   ____ pleasant   ____ tense

2. Check the sentence that best expresses the main idea of this story.

   ____ Charlie attended a kite festival.

   ____ Kites were invented in Asia.

   ____ There are many types of kites.

Write **F** for fact or **O** for opinion before each statement below.

3. ____ Kites are colorful.

4. ____ Kites were invented in Asia.

5. ____ Kites have been used in scientific experiments.

6. ____ A ten-mile-an-hour wind is perfect for kite flying.

7. Check the most likely outcome of this story.

   ____ Charlie will want to attend next year's kite festival.

   ____ Pat will make a kite of her own.

   ____ Pat won't want to attend any more kite festivals.

Learning to Study

Read this classified advertisement from the newspaper and answer the questions below.

For Sale: Flexible silk kite. 8'x10'. $150 firm. Call 555-4553 after 5:00 P.M.

1. What is the cost of the kite? _____

2. What type of kite is it? _____

3. How large is the kite? _____

4. When can you call? _____

Hang Gliding

Read to find out what Pat learns about hang gliding

1   "Now that you've flown an ultralight, you have to try hang gliding," Charlotte said to Pat. It was a beautiful Saturday morning. Charlotte had convinced Pat to come to the hills of Virginia to meet her friend Jane, who could teach them about hang gliding.

2   "What am I doing here?" Pat said half to herself. "First you got me in a glider with no engine, then an ultralight. Now you want me to fly with no protection at all. I'm just an innocent bystander, not a bird."

3   "Come on now, Pat," Jane assured her. "It's really fun and safe if you follow the safety precautions and don't try to do things beyond your skill level.

4   "Hang gliders," Jane continued, "are made of a triangular piece of synthetic cloth connected to an aluminum frame. The cloth acts as a sail. The pilot hangs from a harness and steers the glider with a control bar. Takeoffs are made by running down a hill into the wind. When the sail fills, the craft is airborne."

5   "That's the part that scares me to death," Pat said. "Frankly, I can't understand why anyone would willingly jump off a mile-high mountain cliff to certain death."

6   "If you wear your helmet, sturdy boots, and long pants, you'll be fine," Jane laughed. "You should also follow my motto: 'Don't fly higher than you'd care to fall.'"

7   "In that case," Charlotte said, "Pat would reach about a two-inch altitude!"

8   "Ho, ho, ho," Pat laughed sarcastically. "How new is this hobby, anyhow?"

9   "Well, many people tried to make wings to fly, but in the early 1950s someone patented a new kind of airfoil to put the fun back in flying. This hang glider was easy to make, and before long lots of people were taking to the air," Jane explained.

10   As Pat, Charlotte, and Jane had been talking, they had been walking up a hill. When they neared the top, Jane assembled her hang glider and prepared for takeoff.

11   "I'll take a short flight to demonstrate how it's done," Jane said.

12   Pat and Charlotte watched as Jane ran down the hill and gracefully lifted off into the breeze. Riding an updraft from the hillside, she soared higher and higher. About half an hour later, she landed in a valley where Pat and Charlotte had agreed to meet her.

13   "Pat's ready to try it," Charlotte said. "After you took off, she watched a twelve-year-old girl and later a man in his seventies fearlessly soar into the air."

14   "Yes," Pat said, "it really does look like fun, and besides, if they can do it, so can I. I would be thankful if you two would do me just one little favor."

15   "What's that?" Charlotte and Jane asked in unison.

16   "Talk me out of it!"

Knowing the Words

Write the words from the story that have the meanings below.

1. measures taken to prevent harm _____
   (Par. 3)

2. scornfully _____
   (Par. 8)

3. to have received the right to produce an invention _____
   (Par. 9)

4. agreement _____
   (Par. 15)

Write the words from the story that are synonyms (words that have the same or nearly the same meanings) for these words.

5. persuaded _____
   (Par. 1)

6. honestly _____
   (Par. 5)

Write the phrases from the story that suggest hyperbole or exaggeration and have these intended meanings.

7. jump off a hill

   _____
   (Par. 5)

8. Pat doesn't want to jump very high.

   _____
   (Par. 7)

Working with Words

Many words can use more than one suffix. Write the words that can be formed by adding the suffixes below to these base words. You may have to change the spelling of the base word before adding a suffix.

	-ful	-ly
1. beauty	_____	_____
2. grace	_____	_____
3. fear	_____	_____
4. thank	_____	_____

Reading and Thinking

Write the word that best completes each sentence.

1. Hang gliders are made from aluminum and _____ materials.
   sarcastic   synthetic   innocent

2. I _____ you that you are perfectly right.
   convince   acknowledge   assure

3. Do you think Pat will really try hang gliding? Explain. _____

   _____

Complete each sentence with the correct word from the story.

4. The cloth on a hang glider acts as a

   _____.
   (Par. 4)

5. Pilots can soar higher in a hang glider by riding an _____.
   (Par. 12)

Learning to Study

A library's card catalog or computer reference system gives you three ways to look up information: by author, by title, or by subject. Read this reference and then answer the questions below.

CALL NO:	J890.23
AUTHOR:	Martin, Lise
MAIN TITLE:	Hang Gliding—The Thrill of It!
PUBLISHER:	Window Press, 1995

1. What is the title of this book?

   _____

2. What is the subject? _____

3. How can you find the book on the shelf?

   _____

The Paper Airplane Contest

Discover how a paper airplane contest is judged.

1 Three weeks after her first hang gliding flight, Pat was a judge for the First Paper Airplane Contest at Rogers Middle School. She had been invited to be a judge by the student committee that sponsored the event. They told her that the contest would be held as a special event during the school's science fair. The reason for the contest was that some teachers wanted to give the students who had worked on making paper airplanes the credit they deserved.

2 Sixth, seventh, and eighth graders were welcome to compete. There were three events: distance, design, and endurance. Students could cut or paint any type of paper to make their planes, but they could not use any adhesives.

3 On the day of the contest, Pat got to the school gym early. Already more than one hundred airplanes had been entered. During the next hour, that number tripled.

4 Pat had been chosen to judge the endurance competition. Her job was to launch each plane and with a stopwatch time the duration of each flight.

5 Before the contest, she was busy looking at the creative plane designs. The planes were made of every type of paper she could think of. Some were made of notebook paper, tissue paper, cardboard, posterboard, and waxed paper. Others were constructed out of hamburger wrappers, newspaper, index cards, tracing paper, and even milk carton paper.

6 Some entries looked like miniature aircraft. Others were in the shape of insects and birds. One was even modeled after a pterodactyl. Some of the more unique planes were strange looking human figures.

7 Soon it was time to get down to business. Pat started launching the entries. Some of them crashed the instant she started her stopwatch. Others remained aloft for several seconds. Those that stayed in flight for more than eight seconds became finalists.

8 At last Pat narrowed the entries down to ten finalists. Each plane was flown a second time. The contestants held their breath as Pat timed each flight.

9 At last, each judge announced a winner. Collette Wiener, a sixth grader, had won in the distance category. Her plane had flown ninety feet. A model of a supersonic jet built by Walter Zalka, a seventh grader, won for best design.

10 Pat was the last judge to take the floor. The winner for endurance was Lin Wong, a sixth grader. Lin's plane had flown for twelve seconds. That time beat the record set at the Second Great International Paper Airplane Contest. That contest had been held in Seattle in 1986.

11 In the end, the contest sponsors took the winning planes to display them at city hall. That same day everyone, including Pat, immediately started a design for next year's contest.

Knowing the Words

Write the words from the story that have the meanings below.

1. contest _____
   (Par. 4)

2. length of time
   that something lasts _____
   (Par. 4)

3. inventive _____
   (Par. 5)

4. contestants in
   the last stage
   of competition _____
   (Par. 7)

5. group of things _____
   (Par. 9)

Write the words from the story that are antonyms (words that mean the opposite) of these words.

6. oversized _____
   (Par. 6)

7. hide _____
   (Par. 11)

8. except for _____
   (Par. 11)

In each row below, circle the two words that are related.

9. cardboard   newspaper   adhesives

10. category   contest   competition

11. event   fair   science

12. Write the meaning of the idiom *take the floor* from paragraph 10.

   _____

Working with Words

Write the compound words from the story that are formed by adding to these words.

1. watch _____
   (Par. 4)

2. book _____
   (Par. 5)

3. card _____
   (Par. 5)

4. news _____
   (Par. 5)

Reading and Thinking

1. Number the events to show the order in which they happened.

   _____ Pat announced the endurance winner.

   _____ Pat tried hang gliding.

   _____ Pat chose the finalists.

   _____ The winning planes were put on display.

   _____ Pat looked at the designs.

   _____ The distance and design winners were announced.

2. Check the sentence that best expresses the main idea of this story.

   _____ There were many creative entries in the paper airplane contest.

   _____ Pat acted as judge for a local paper airplane contest.

   _____ There were three events in the paper airplane contest.

3. Check the most likely conclusion you can make as to why the paper airplane contest was held.

   _____ Teachers wanted to encourage paper airplane making.

   _____ Teachers didn't like students making paper airplanes in class.

   _____ Teachers thought a contest would be a good way to turn a game into a learning experience.

Learning to Study

Check the information that is necessary in an announcement for a paper airplane contest.

_____ judges' names   _____ place of contest

_____ contest rules   _____ contest sponsor

_____ previous   _____ news of other
      winners   contests

Airplanes for Everyone

Read to see how many kinds of model planes are mentioned.

1   Charlie had just finished dinner when his doorbell rang.

2   "Hi, Charlie!" said Stewart and Ramon, two of the children who live in Charlie's apartment building. "Are you busy?"

3   "No," said Charlie. "What's up?"

4   "Well, I was flying my plane at the school, and I had a minor accident," explained Stewart anxiously.

5   "A minor accident! This thing is in pieces," Charlie exclaimed as he carefully took the airplane model from his young friend. "Let's take it into the workroom."

6   As he switched on the light, Stewart's and Ramon's eyes lit up, too. What they saw was a room filled with airplane models of all sizes and descriptions. Some were in display cases, others were on bookshelves, and several hung from the ceiling.

7   "Did you make these yourself?" asked Ramon.

8   "Yes," Charlie answered. "It's taken a long time, but doing each step just right is the fun of it."

9   "I'm interested to know if you ever enter them in contests?" said Stewart.

10   "No, but many people do," Charlie said. "There are clubs that hold contests, even international ones, all the time. Some are for miniature display models like mine. The models are judged on how well they are made and how closely they duplicate real planes.

11   "Other contests are for both indoor and outdoor flying models," Charlie continued. "The indoor planes are usually quite fragile. Most often they are made of balsa wood. They are propelled by tightening rubber bands around the propellers.

12   "Some outdoor planes are gliders. Others have engines," Charlie went on.

13   "Engines!" interrupted Ramon. "What keeps them under control? Why don't they just fly off?"

14   "Sometimes they do," Charlie laughed. "But if everything's in working order, that doesn't happen too often. Several models have timers that shut off the engines after the plane is aloft, so the planes can glide for a while. Other planes, called control-line models, fly at the ends of wires that control the plane's altitude and flight path. Also, there are radio-controlled models that use a transmitter to direct the plane's flight."

15   As Charlie had been talking, he had been working on Stewart's plane, an outdoor glider with a two-foot wingspread. "If you have enough patience to let your glider dry overnight, it should be fixed," he said as he finished gluing the wing in place.

16   "That's fine," said Stewart. "Thanks a million, Charlie."

17   "Yes, thanks for letting us see your workshop, Charlie," Ramon added. "This has given me a terrific idea for a report I have to do in school on hobbies. I think I've just finished my first interview."

Knowing the Words

Write the words from the story that have the meanings below.

1. copy _____
   (Par. 10)

2. delicate _____
   (Par. 11)

3. lightweight wood _____
   (Par. 11)

4. model airplane
   that is guided
   by wires _____
   (Par. 14)

5. device for
   sending messages _____
   (Par. 14)

6. calm endurance _____
   (Par. 15)

Write the words from the story that are represented by these abbreviations.

7. apt. _____
   (Par. 2)

8. bldg. _____
   (Par. 2)

9. sch. _____
   (Par. 4)

10. cont. _____
    (Par. 11)

Working with Words

The prefix **inter-** means "between" or "among." Write the words from the story that have the prefix **inter-** and come from these base words.

1. nation _____
   (Par. 10)

2. view _____
   (Par. 17)

Match the words that have the prefix **inter-** with the meanings below.

   a. intersection   c. intermission
   b. interrupted   d. interfere

3. _____ pause between acts

4. _____ place where two things cross

5. _____ meddle

6. _____ broke into an ongoing activity

Reading and Thinking

1. Do you think Ramon's report will be a good one? Explain.

   _____

2. Why did Stewart take his broken airplane model to Charlie?

   _____

Write **F** for fact or **O** for opinion before each statement below.

3. _____ Some model airplanes are gliders.

4. _____ Radio-control models are the best.

5. _____ There is more than one kind of contest for model airplanes.

6. _____ Some models could win prizes.

7. Check the word that best describes Ramon.

   _____ impatient   _____ funny

   _____ quiet   _____ interested

Learning to Study

A chart helps to organize and compare information by using words or numbers. Study the chart that Ramon made for his report and then answer the questions below.

Model Airplanes	Engine Types
Display	None
Indoor	Rubber Band
Free-Flight	Rubber Band or Piston
Control-Line	Piston or Jet
Radio-Control	Electric

1. How many types of model airplanes did Ramon discover? _____

2. Why is there no engine type for Display models? _____

3. What four types of engines do model airplanes use?

   _____

Skydiving

Read to find out what it's like to make a parachute jump.

1 "Do you know how to make a parachute jump?" Pat asked Charlotte.

2 "Not quite yet," Charlotte answered.

3 "Say, 'Boo!'" joked Pat. At last Pat had found an aerial sport that Charlotte had not yet tried. Today Pat and Charlie were going to witness Charlotte's first jump.

4 As a pilot, Pat knew the value of knowing how to use a parachute in case of an emergency. She was not interested, as Charlotte was, in skydiving for pleasure. "I just don't see the need for making a ten thousand-foot jump if it's not absolutely necessary," Pat had explained.

5 Charlotte had completed a full day of training and was ready to jump. Her first leap would be done on a static line, which is a line that attaches the parachute to the plane. Just after she would jump from the plane, the chute would open automatically. She wore a helmet, coveralls, goggles, and boots for protection.

6 In addition, she had two different chutes. Her main chute was strapped to her back. The reserve chute was attached to her chest, to be used if the main chute failed to open. Charlotte also had a stopwatch and an instrument for measuring altitude.

7 Although she was nervous as the plane neared the target area at three thousand feet, she was excited, too. Two others were jumping that afternoon, and all of them had butterflies in their stomachs. When it was her turn, Charlotte took a deep breath and jumped boldly.

8 From the very beginning, she loved it! Her short free-fall was a sensation that was truly unique. She felt like a bird flying over the earth. To her surprise, there was no great shock when the chute opened. The feeling was similar to one you might have on an elevator that stops quickly on its way down. Charlotte floated gently to the ground, and when she landed, she rolled sideways. The soft landing spread the shock throughout her body to prevent injury.

9 "Well, are you ready for another jump?" Pat inquired, when Charlotte arrived back at the airport. She and Charlie honestly expected Charlotte to be nervous, like most people after their first jump, and beg off.

10 "Ready? I positively can't wait!" Charlotte exclaimed. "When I've made five more jumps, I'll be allowed to pull my own ripcord. How many more do you figure I can make today?"

11 "I can't believe it," Pat said under her breath. "If somebody doesn't knock some sense into you, you'll have your expert's license before the week is over."

Knowing the Words

Write the words from the story that have the meanings below.

1. having to do
   with the air _____
   (Par. 3)

2. sport of
   parachute jumping _____
   (Par. 4)

3. cord attached from
   airplane to parachute _____
   (Par. 5)

4. dropping before the
   parachute opens _____
   (Par. 8)

5. string that is pulled
   to open a parachute _____
   (Par. 10)

Write the meanings of the idioms in this story.

6. *butterflies in their stomachs*

   _____

7. *beg off* _____

8. *knock some sense into*

   _____

9. Find the simile in paragraph 8 and write it below.

   _____

Working with Words

Rewrite each of the phrases below. Use possessive forms.

1. the first jump of Charlotte

   _____

2. the licenses of the experts

   _____

3. the biggest challenge of aviation

   _____

Reading and Thinking

1. Check the most likely reason the author had for writing this story.

   _____ to train people to skydive

   _____ to introduce the reader to a sport

   _____ to make people go to air shows

2. Check the word that best describes the mood of this story.

   _____ astonishment   _____ seriousness

   _____ excitement   _____ fearfulness

Write the word that best completes each sentence.

3. There was _____ nothing else to do but jump.

   automatically   absolutely   gently

4. When the _____ opened, she was relieved.

   chute   ripcord   static line

Learning to Study

Many words have more than one meaning. Dictionaries number the definitions after each entry. Use a dictionary to find two meanings for each word below.

1. class

   _____   _____

2. elevator

   _____   _____

3. Complete this partial outline of paragraph 8.

   I. Parachute jump

       A. _____

       B. _____

       C. _____

Careers in Aviation

Read to see how many different jobs you can find in this story.

1   Each day thousands of planes filled with passengers and cargo climb into the sky. It takes the combined effort of many men and women to make this happen. This community of workers has as its goal safe and smooth air travel.

2   At the airport terminal, airline company workers communicate with travelers. They make reservations, sell tickets, check baggage, and give flight information.

3   Getting the planes ready is the job of still more men and women. They are called the turnaround crew. The turnaround crew

quickly cleans each plane between flights. At the same time, ramp crew members load freight and baggage into the cargo area of the plane. Trucks carrying meals and water also deliver to the waiting plane at this time.

4   Planes must also be refueled. Fuel may be delivered by huge tank trucks or pumped in from underground tanks. Computers speed up the flow of fuel from underground tanks. The refueling process takes only about ten minutes.

5   In the midst of all this commotion, work of the most important kind is being done. Mechanics fix any problems reported by the flight crew. They wash the plane's windshield and change the oil. In less than forty minutes, turnaround is completed and it's time for the passengers to board.

6   After the plane has been boarded, the ground controller directs the pilot to where the plane will take off. When the plane is in position, the air controller OKs the takeoff.

7   Other people work to ensure safe landings and takeoffs. The maintenance crew keeps runways clean all year long. They keep them clear of snow and stones or other things that could puncture a tire or cause a plane to jolt. They repair holes or bumps in the runways and check on the many kinds of lights that are used to outline the runways. Some airports even have a crew responsible for making sure birds stay away from the area because they can cause engines to stall or break windshields.

8   In the hangar, a group of mechanics like Pat's friend Carol works to make sure that the planes stay in top shape. Their job is to care for the engines, aircraft structure, and all of the equipment. Each plane is given a complete overhaul on a regular schedule.

9   All these jobs are vital to the smooth, efficient running of an airport. Besides those mentioned here, however, many more careers can be found in the field of aviation.

Photograph by Mark Segal / Tony Stone Images

Knowing the Words

Write the words from the story that have the meanings below.

1. series of actions _____ (Par. 4)

2. disturbance _____ (Par. 5)

3. director _____ (Par. 6)

4. not wasting time or effort _____ (Par. 9)

5. Check the sentence in which *outline* has the same meaning as in paragraph 7.

   ____ Do you see the cat's outline?

   ____ Trees outline the landscape.

   ____ Write an outline before you begin writing your article.

Some words can be written in more than one way, depending on their meaning. For example, *take off* is a verb showing action, but *takeoff* is a noun. Complete each sentence with *take off* or *takeoff.*

6. The plane will _____ on time.

7. The pilot's _____ was perfect.

Working with Words

The prefix **com-** means "with" or "together." Write the words from the story that have the prefix **com-** and come from these foreign base words.

1. from Latin *bini,* meaning "two by two" _____ (Par. 1)

2. from Latin *munus,* meaning "service" _____ (Par. 1)

3. from Latin *movēre,* meaning "to move" _____ (Par. 5)

Reading and Thinking

1. Check the sentence that best expresses the main idea of this story.

   ____ Passengers fly around the world.

   ____ Many people run an airport.

   ____ The turnaround crew gets each plane ready for takeoff.

2. In what ways can a plane be refueled?

   _____

   _____

3. Summarize the information in paragraph 3 in one sentence.

   _____

   _____

Learning to Study

Below is a help-wanted ad from the classified section of a newspaper. Read the ad and then answer the questions below.

Airplane Mechanic: 2 yrs. exper. with planes necessary. Must be willing to relocate. 555-4469.

1. Should people who have no mechanical experience apply for this job? Why?

   _____

2. Should people who want to move apply for this job? Why?

   _____

A dictionary entry word's part of speech is often indicated by an abbreviation that follows the respelling. Use a dictionary to match these words to their parts of speech.

3. ____ mechanic   **a.** preposition

4. ____ carefully   **b.** adjective

5. ____ of   **c.** noun

6. ____ important   **d.** adverb

7. ____ communicate   **e.** verb

Career in the Clouds

Read to see what types of things a flight attendant must know.

1   Pat's college friend Arnie is a flight attendant for a large airline. Thirty years ago it would have been unusual to find a man with this job. At that time, for the most part, airlines hired only single women as flight attendants. Today, however, both single and married men and women are flight attendants. Each month, Arnie makes five round-trip flights between New York and Paris. It sounds exciting, doesn't it? But it's hard work, too.

2   Before takeoff, Arnie makes himself familiar with the flight conditions and the flight schedule. He checks the cabin, the food, and the safety gear. He greets people when they board the plane. Although most flights are uneventful, he reviews safety procedures with the passengers. Arnie identifies the exits and describes the use of oxygen masks. Since the plane will fly over water, he explains how to use life jackets and rafts. The last thing Arnie has to do before the plane takes off is check for loose baggage in the cabin.

3   In flight, Arnie makes sure the people in his section are comfortable and safe. He provides blankets, pillows, magazines, and meals. He answers questions about the flight and traveling in France. He gives special care to children and inexperienced travelers. He is prepared for medical or air emergencies.

4   Arnie, a college graduate, is fluent in a second language. That is important for international flight attendants. He had six weeks of training at the airline's flight training center. Here he learned the standards for personal appearance and attitude. He received first aid training and was taught what to do in case of an emergency landing. Arnie also received special training in the rules for passports and customs. Each year, Arnie must get about fourteen more hours of training in dealing with emergencies and passengers.

5   The number of flight attendants on a plane depends on the plane size and flight length. On small planes, there may be only one attendant. On large international flights there may be as many as fifteen.

6   Arnie flies about seventy-five hours a month. Then he spends another seventy-five hours preparing for flights and writing reports after a flight.

7   There are a number of job benefits for Arnie. He and his family get discounts on air fares. He also gets paid vacations, insurance benefits, and extra pay for working overtime.

8   "I love my job!" Arnie admits. "Of course, there have been some turbulent times. We've had bad weather, engine problems, and rowdy passengers. Still, I don't want to do anything else because this job gives me the chance to travel and meet new people. Also, I get to keep my head in the clouds without getting into trouble!"

Knowing the Words

Write the words from the story that have the meanings below.

1. waits on others _____
   (Par. 1)

2. ways of doing things _____
   (Par. 2)

3. smooth and rapid _____
   (Par. 4)

4. between countries _____
   (Par. 4)

5. stormy or disorderly _____
   (Par. 8)

Write the words from the story that are synonyms (words that have the same or nearly the same meanings) for these words.

6. odd _____
   (Par. 1)

7. luggage _____
   (Par. 2)

8. untrained _____
   (Par. 3)

9. noisy _____
   (Par. 8)

10. Check the sentence in which *checks* has the same meaning as in paragraph 2.

    ____ I marked the papers with checks.

    ____ We have a system of checks and balances.

    ____ She checks the baby hourly.

Working with Words

Both a prefix and a suffix can be added to many words. Write the words that can be created by adding the given prefix and suffix to each of the following base words.

Base	Prefix	Suffix	
1. nation	inter-	-al	_____
2. usual	un-	-ly	_____
3. event	un-	-ful	_____
4. friend	un-	-ly	_____

Reading and Thinking

1. Number the following events to show the order in which they happen on a flight.

   ____ Passengers are directed to seats.

   ____ The plane takes off.

   ____ The attendant checks the supplies.

   ____ Meals are served.

   ____ Safety procedures are reviewed.

   ____ The cabin is checked for loose baggage.

2. Check the most likely reason the author had for writing this story.

   ____ to describe a man named Arnie

   ____ to describe a plane ride

   ____ to describe an attendant's job

3. What second language do you think Arnie speaks fluently? _____

4. Check the words that describe a good flight attendant.

   ____ shy   ____ rowdy

   ____ friendly   ____ helpful

   ____ efficient   ____ calm

Learning to Study

1. Complete this outline of the headings for paragraphs 2–4 of this story.

   I. _____

   II. _____

   III. _____

2. Check the references you might use to find out more about a career as a flight attendant.

   ____ atlas   ____ card catalog

   ____ thesaurus   ____ *Readers' Guide*

   ____ almanac   ____ encyclopedia

How Are Airplanes Tested?

Read to find out how airplanes are designed and tested.

1   Not all jobs in aviation require flying in an airplane. Many scientists and engineers who design and test planes never leave the ground. You might say they build and fly model airplanes for a living. Even though this sounds like fun, it's serious business.

2   The cargo company for which Pat works just bought a brand-new plane. An engineer who worked on the new plane was asked to talk to all the pilots about the aircraft's design. Alex Scholl, the chief engineer, came to Vista headquarters and explained the new plane's features. After his talk, some pilots asked about the testing of the new plane. Alex was a good one to ask since he had worked on this plane from the start.

3   He said that first the engineers had to come up with a blueprint of the plane design. To do this, a computer was programmed with detailed descriptions or the specifications of the new plane. The computer designed a mathematical model. Next, the computer was programmed with atmospheric data. The computer then could test how the plane might react in flight.

4   Alex said the next step was to build a model of the new plane. The model matched the computer design. The model was only one-tenth the size of the real plane. It was then tested in a wind tunnel.

5   A wind tunnel has three parts: a fan, a tunnel for the wind to blow through, and a control room. The fan can send wind through the tunnel at low or supersonic speeds. The temperature and the air pressure can be controlled, too. The wind tunnel tests helped the engineers find out what would happen when the plane flew at different altitudes, speeds, or weather conditions. These tests were done many times as changes were made in the design.

6   Next the plane itself was constructed. The scientists tested the structure with heat, sound waves, weight, and vibration. Electronic tests were run on all of the equipment as well.

7   At last flight tests were performed. Specially trained test pilots flew the plane and observed and reported its responses. They started with ground taxi tests. Then they did brief flight tests. At last they did longer flight tests.

8   Alex explained that the testing program took several years to complete. It involved hundreds of people who had to be responsible each step of the way. Designers, scientists, engineers, and test pilots all played important roles in the process. "You can see the results of all of our efforts when these new planes fly overhead," he said. "From idea to model to finished aircraft, they passed each test with flying colors."

Knowing the Words

Write the words from the story that have the meanings below.

1. people who plan and build things _____ (Par. 1)

2. detailed descriptions _____ (Par. 3)

3. information or facts _____ (Par. 3)

4. respond _____ (Par. 3)

5. shaking motion _____ (Par. 6)

6. dealing with science that makes computers, radios, and radar work _____ (Par. 6)

Write the words from the story that are antonyms (words that mean the opposite) of these words.

7. destructed _____ (Par. 6)

8. under _____ (Par. 8)

In each row below, circle the two words that are related.

9. built   constructed   reacted

10. model   equipment   blueprint

11. What does the idiom *passed with flying colors* mean in paragraph 8?

_____

Working with Words

The prefix **ir-** means "not." Write the meaning of each word below.

1. irregular _____

2. irresponsible _____

3. irresistible _____

4. irreplaceable _____

5. irreversible _____

Reading and Thinking

1. Why do you think the pilots wanted to know how the planes were tested?

_____

2. In one sentence, summarize the information in paragraph 3.

_____

_____

3. Check the types of airplane tests that are in the story.

____ computer test   ____ history test

____ wind test   ____ flight test

____ electronic test   ____ science test

Write the word that best completes each sentence.

4. The airplane's _____ will be programmed into a computer.

   specifications   models   blueprints

5. The computer created the first

   _____ model of the plane.

   atmospheric   mathematical   economical

Learning to Study

Match each reference source below with the kind of information it might contain.

a. atlas   **b.** dictionary   **c.** *Readers' Guide*

d. encyclopedia   **e.** newspaper   **f.** almanac

1. ____ a short definition of *blueprint*

2. ____ the name of a magazine article on recent aircraft design

3. ____ today's temperature in Denver

4. ____ a complete history of aeronautical engineering

5. ____ a map of Houston, Texas

6. ____ aircraft speed records

A View from the Air

Look for the many uses that are made of aerial pictures.

1   Waiting for his flight after a vacation with his family in Arizona, Charlie saw somebody he remembered from flight school.

2   "Charlie?" she asked uncertainly.

3   "You're Joanna Orland, aren't you?" Charlie exclaimed.

4   "It's been at least twenty years," Joanna laughed. "What have you been doing?"

5   "I'm a cargo pilot," Charlie answered. "I've been with the same company since I left the Air Force. I've been on vacation and now I'm on my way back to work. How about you?"

6   Joanna's eyes lit up as she answered, "Well, I have a lot to tell you. I was a commuter airline pilot in New York for several years. It so happened that one of my regular passengers, Evan, was a well-known aerial photographer. He told me all about his job. It seemed like the perfect occupation for me. It combined aviation with my favorite hobby, photography.

7   "For a few years I had taken aerial shots for fun. I showed some of them to Evan. He liked them and recommended me for some temporary work. My first job was taking pictures for a mapmaking service."

8   "This is really interesting," said Charlie. "Tell me more."

9   Joanna smiled and said, "My next job was taking pictures for a forestry service. They used aerial pictures to spot diseased trees. They also used them to choose some new campgrounds and locate natural resources. After that I changed jobs.

10   "Evan had decided to start his own business. He asked me to be his partner in the business and in real life, too. We were married ten years ago.

11   "We've been lucky. We've done aerial surveys for researchers who want to track animals. We've taken photographs for archaeologists who are looking for new sites. Also, we've done a lot of jobs for cities. Our shots let cities study pollution and potential traffic problems.

12   "Two years ago, we bought an infrared camera that can photograph different temperatures. Now our pictures can show how much heat is escaping from buildings.

13   "The most exciting job we've had," she continued, "was taking pictures of an active volcano in Hawaii. Evan and I were so thrilled, we didn't realize how close we got to the heat. When we landed, we noticed that the helicopter runners had been burned."

14   "Wow!" said Charlie. "I'm impressed. It sounds as if you have a great job."

15   "I love it!" said Joanna. "As a matter of fact, I'm waiting for Evan to fly in from the East Coast. We're headed up to take some shots of the Grand Canyon."

16   At that moment, their conversation was interrupted by the announcement of Charlie's flight. "Looks as if I'm on my way," he said. "It was great to see you, Joanna. Good luck with your expedition."

17   "Thanks," Joanna replied. "Maybe I'll see you in another twenty years!"

Knowing the Words

Write the words from the story that have the meanings below.

1. career _____
   (Par. 6)

2. available supplies _____
   (Par. 9)

3. those who study
   ancient things _____
   (Par. 11)

4. possible _____
   (Par. 11)

5. invisible rays _____
   (Par. 12)

Write the words from the story that are represented by these abbreviations.

6. AZ _____
   (Par. 1)

7. sch. _____
   (Par. 1)

8. co. _____
   (Par. 5)

9. NY _____
   (Par. 6)

10. photog. _____
    (Par. 6)

11. temp. _____
    (Par. 12)

12. HI _____
    (Par. 13)

13. Check the sentence in which *spot* has the same meaning as in paragraph 9.

    _____ I have a spot on my sleeve.

    _____ I can spot a mistake.

    _____ From this spot, I can see it.

Working with Words

Write the closed and hyphenated compound words from the story that are formed by adding words to these words.

1. body _____
   (Par. 1)

2. known _____
   (Par. 6)

3. map _____
   (Par. 7)

4. camp _____
   (Par. 9)

Reading and Thinking

1. Check the sentence that best expresses the main idea of this story.

   _____ Aerial photographers make maps.

   _____ Aerial photography has a lot of uses.

   _____ Archaeologists use aerial photos.

2. Why is it helpful for people to know if heat is escaping from buildings?

   _____

3. What might be some future uses of aerial photographs?

   _____

   _____

Learning to Study

Sometimes the spelling of a base word changes when an ending is added. In this case, a dictionary will give the irregular spelling in its entry. Use a dictionary to find the irregular spelling of the words below that have **-ed** and **-ing** added.

	-ed	-ing
1. realize	_____	_____
2. improve	_____	_____
3. overlap	_____	_____
4. plan	_____	_____

5. Complete this outline of paragraph 11.

   I. Uses of Aerial Photography

      A. _____

      B. _____

      C. _____

      D. _____

Smoke Jumpers

Read to find out why it's easier to control forest fires now than it was years ago.

1   Forest fires are all too common from spring through fall. Lightning and unattended campfires often start fires in places that are very difficult for firefighters to reach. There are several ways forest fires are spotted in these areas. Lookouts in fire towers, fire spotters in airplanes, and satellites that can sense hot areas are used to find fires in these places. Computers relay information on weather and soil conditions quickly, saving valuable time.

2   The phone rang at the station. It was the lookout reporting a fire. Looking at a map of the park, John Pearce, the fire chief, groaned. He wished the lookout had seen an illusion. There were no roads into that area. Firefighters would need a whole day to get to that place. It was illogical to think that the fire would contain itself. If quick action was not taken, the fire would become a raging giant.

3   The alarm sounded. First the park's crew went out. Bulldozers started clearing away anything that would burn. Within half

an hour, a big plane zeroed in on the fire. It dipped over the forest at the outer rim of the smoke. Parachutists jumped from the plane. The smoke jumpers were coming to the rescue.

4   These parachuting firefighters wore special safety equipment. Each padded suit was fireproof and had a stiff collar to protect the neck. A crash helmet and a face guard protected against tree branches. Each jumper carried about eighty pounds of equipment. This included a two-way radio, a shovel, and an aluminum heat shield. The heat shield is a tent that firefighters can unfold and crawl into if the fire comes too close. The plane circled again, and more parachutes opened. Drifting down were food, water, and other fire-fighting tools.

5   Other planes with chemical sprays were on alert to help in case the smoke jumpers could not control the fire.

6   On the ground, the smoke jumpers got busy right away digging a fire line. This is a trench that surrounds the fire to keep it from spreading. Meanwhile, helicopters with large buckets carried thousands of gallons of water to cool down areas so the firefighters could work. Elsewhere, tanker planes carrying three thousand gallons of water were working to put out the fire.

7   The smoke jumpers worked hard for eight hours straight. By digging a circle around the fire with their shovels, they had tamed the wild lion. Now they would head back to their base to check and repair their equipment.

8   Back at headquarters, John and everyone else felt relieved. The new system had worked again, and hundreds of trees, which years ago would have been lost, had been saved. Getting the right people to the right place in a hurry really made the difference.

Knowing the Words

Write the words from the story that have the meanings below.

1. pass along _____
   (Par. 1)

2. something not real _____
   (Par. 2)

3. not reasonable _____
   (Par. 2)

4. ditch _____
   (Par. 6)

Write the metaphors from the story.

5. _____
   (Par. 2)

6. _____
   (Par. 7)

7. Check the sentence in which *contain* has the same meaning as in paragraph 2.

   ____ She could not contain her laughter when she heard the joke.

   ____ Encyclopedias contain facts.

   ____ This jar can contain liquid.

Working with Words

The prefixe **il-** means "not." Form the antonym, or opposite, of the words below by adding the prefix **il-** to each one.

1. logical _____

2. legal _____

3. legible _____

Compound words can be open, closed, or hyphenated. Write the compound words from the story that are formed by adding words to these words.

4. towers _____
   (Par. 1)

5. out _____
   (Par. 2)

6. two _____
   (Par. 4)

7. quarters _____
   (Par. 8)

Reading and Thinking

1. Number the events to show the order in which they happened.

   ____ Bulldozers cleared a path.

   ____ A fire alarm sounded.

   ____ A fire was out of control.

   ____ Helicopters dropped buckets of water.

   ____ Smoke jumpers reached the fire.

   ____ Everyone at headquarters felt relieved.

Write **B** before the statements that describe events that happened before the smoke jumpers arrived. Write **A** before statements that describe events that occurred after they arrived.

2. ____ A lookout spotted a fire.

3. ____ Planes dropped water on the fire.

4. ____ A fire line was dug.

5. ____ The commander looked over the situation.

6. Check the sentence that best expresses the main idea of this story.

   ____ Fires can be fought on land and from the air.

   ____ Firefighters have a risky job.

   ____ Fire destroys hundreds of acres of trees each year.

Learning to Study

Refer to the pronunciation key on the inside back cover of this book. Write the word that each of these respellings represents.

1. /si chə wā´ shən/ _____

2. /zē´ rōd/ _____

3. /rē´ lā/ _____

4. /i kwip´mənt/ _____

Bush Pilots

Read to find out why bush pilots have been so important to Alaskan life.

1   One of flying's more thrilling occupations is that of bush pilot. The word *bush* in this case doesn't mean "shrub." It means "wilderness." That tells where bush pilots fly. They fly into wilderness areas. Before and after the Second World War, Charlie's Uncle Leonard was a bush pilot. When Charlie was a boy, he heard all about his uncle's adventures in the wilderness of Alaska. He knew that from the start of modern aviation, bush pilots had been essential to the people of the state.

2   Alaska has the largest land area of any state in the United States. Its terrain consists of many mountains, rivers, and forests. Building roads or railroads is difficult because many areas are hard to reach. Also, construction seasons are short, and the severe winters are hard on the highways that do exist.

3   Given all of these facts, what do you think is the best way to travel in Alaska? If you said by airplane, you'd be right.

4   From the early days of flying, long before Alaska became a state in 1959, planes linked its remote places to the rest of the world. This type of flying is what lured Charlie's uncle from his home. He was a young pilot looking for adventure.

5   Before World War II, flying had a large element of risk no matter where you were. But in Alaska there was always more pressure. The weather was a major consideration. Leonard might fly in frigid weather more than fifty degrees below zero. He flew into some towns where the main streets served as runways for his plane.

6   Leonard brought supplies and news to remote areas. He might carry mail or medicine. Often his passengers were victims of illnesses or accidents who were being rushed to doctors. Bush pilots routinely risked their lives for others.

7   Today some of the circumstances in Alaska have changed. There are more than seven hundred fifty airports in the state. From them, bush pilots make flights for both scheduled and emergency trips. Many bush pilots still carry people to hospitals and deliver mail to remote areas. Many others operate air taxis.

8   That is what Charlie's cousin does. She runs a flightseeing business. She shows tourists the amazing sights this state has to offer. Each summer thousands of tourists get a view of Alaska's natural wonders.

9   Although the role of the bush pilot has changed somewhat, Alaska's state motto, "North to the Future," still fits those fearless pilots who want to "test their wings."

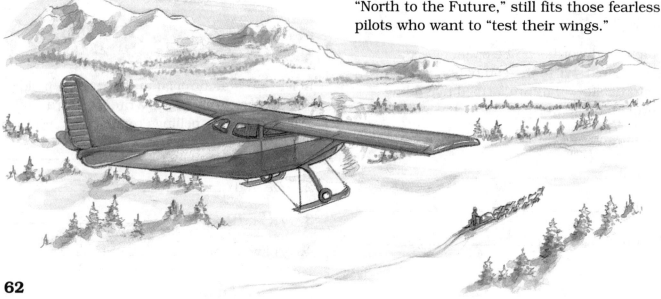

Knowing the Words

Write the words from the story that have the meanings below.

1. necessary _____
   (Par. 1)

2. landscape _____
   (Par. 2)

3. tempted _____
   (Par. 4)

4. very cold _____
   (Par. 5)

Write the words from the story that are synonyms (words that have the same or nearly the same meanings) for these words.

5. wilderness _____
   (Par. 1)

6. unafraid _____
   (Par. 9)

Learning to Study

Use this chart to answer these questions.

Wind Speed (mph)	Air Temperature (F°)			
	35°	25°	15°	5°
	Wind Chill Temperature			
4	35°	25°	15°	5°
5	32°	22°	11°	0°
10	22°	10°	−3°	−15°
15	16°	2°	−11°	−25°
20	12°	−3°	−17°	−31°

1. What is the wind chill temperature when wind speed is 15 mph and air

   temperature is 15°? _____

2. What is the temperature if wind chill is

   -31° and wind speed is 20 mph? _____

3. What is the wind speed if the wind chill

   is 11° and the temperature is 15°? _____

4. Check the best sources for finding out about bush pilots.

   ____ telephone books   ____ card catalog

   ____ *Readers' Guide*   ____ atlas

   ____ encyclopedia   ____ dictionary

Reading and Thinking

Write two of the reasons that tell why it is hard to travel in Alaska.

1. _____

2. _____

3. Why is being a bush pilot dangerous?

   _____

4. Will air travel always be vital to Alaska?

   Explain. _____

Write **F** for fact or **O** for opinion before each statement below.

5. ____ Bush pilots have risky jobs.

6. ____ Alaska became a state in 1959.

7. ____ Alaska is the largest state.

8. ____ Flying is difficult in Alaska.

Write the word that best completes each sentence.

9. Under these _____ we had no choice but to jump from the plane.

   departures   circumstances   frontiers

10. A big _____ in choosing clothes is the wind chill temperature.

    beginning   wilderness   consideration

Working with Words

The suffix **-ure** means "act or process of." Write the words that have the suffix **-ure** and these meanings below. You may have to drop the final *e* in the base word before adding the suffix.

1. act of pressing _____

2. act of departing _____

3. act of exposing _____

Autopilot

Read to find out how an autopilot works.

1   "Well, we're cruising now," Charlie said. "Let's switch over to autopilot and have some lunch." Charlie and Pat were making a transcontinental flight. They were bringing produce from the West Coast to the East.

2   "Sounds good to me," said Pat. "That autopilot is a wonderful invention. It's good to know it can steer the plane better than we can. I just hope it won't make us obsolete."

3   "Well, maybe you'll be obsolete, but they could never replace me," Charlie laughed. "You know, I heard that another plane flying late at night missed Los Angeles by a hundred miles because the pilots fell asleep. The air traffic controllers had to awaken them by shouting over the radio."

4   "That's pretty scary," Pat said. "Everyone on that plane could have been a dead duck."

5   The autopilot that Pat and Charlie discussed is a device that can steer an airplane or a ship. An autopilot has a gyroscope that is more exact than a toy gyroscope, but it works the same way.

6   A gyroscope is a rapidly spinning top. It is set in a frame that lets it tilt in any direction. The word *gyroscope* comes from the Greek words *gyros,* meaning "rotation," and *skopein,* meaning "to view." When you pull the wound-up string on a toy gyroscope, its wheel starts to spin. If you set it down, the spinning wheel stays in the same place even if you move the frame.

7   In an airplane's autopilot, more precise wheels can be set on a certain course. They will maintain that course as the plane moves. One gyroscope controls the plane's ailerons and elevators. It keeps the nose of the plane from moving up and down or from dipping to one side or the other. The second gyroscope controls the plane's rudder. It keeps the plane's nose from moving sideways.

8   Because it is so precise, an autopilot can steer a plane closer to its course than a human pilot can. This allows the pilots to do other things knowing the plane will stay on course. An autopilot can only be a problem if the pilot sets the wrong course or if there is an equipment breakdown. However, for the most part autopilots are a great advance for aviation.

9   Autopilots were tested in airplanes only ten years after the first planes were in the air. In 1933, an autopilot helped Wiley Post make a solo flight around the world.

10   Pat said, "Well, an autopilot can fly better than we can. It reacts quicker than we do. But there's one thing it can't do that you do quite well, Charlie."

11   "What's that?" Charlie asked.

12   "Argue with me!" laughed Pat.

Knowing the Words

Write the words from the story that have the meanings below.

1. no longer useful _____
   (Par. 2)

2. instrument with a
   spinning wheel
   inside a frame _____
   (Par. 5)

3. exact _____
   (Par. 7)

4. responds _____
   (Par. 10)

Write the words from the story that are synonyms (words that have the same or nearly the same meanings) for these words.

5. instrument _____
   (Par. 5)

6. failure _____
   (Par. 8)

Learning to Study

1. Complete this outline of paragraph 7.

   I. What an autopilot contols
       A. One gyroscope

           1. _____

           2. _____

       B. Second gyroscope

           1. _____

Read this airline ticket and then answer the questions below.

Passenger Name			Date of Issue	
Price, Elizabeth			12 Jan 97	
	Flight	**Class**	**Date**	**Time**
FROM: Nashville	4403	C	1Mar	540P
TO: Little Rock	4403	C	1Mar	840P

2. When was the ticket issued? _____

3. Where is Elizabeth going? _____

4. How long is the flight? _____

5. On what date is she traveling? _____

Reading and Thinking

1. Why won't pilots become obsolete?

   _____

2. What problem can occur if a pilot naps while the autopilot is in control?

   _____

3. Check the sentence that best expresses the main idea of this story.

   ____ Autopilots are better than human pilots.

   ____ An autopilot is a device that can steer a plane.

   ____ Autopilots are like toy gyroscopes.

4. Check the most likely reason the author had for writing this story.

   ____ to explain what an autopilot is

   ____ to explain autopilot problems

   ____ to explain why autopilots are better than human pilots

Write the word that best completes each sentence.

5. The toy _____ spun for over a minute.

   course   gyroscope   advance

6. The pilot set a _____ for New Orleans.

   gyroscope   cockpit   course

Working with Words

Use the possessive form of the word in parentheses in each sentence.

1. The _____ lives are in the hands of the pilot. (group)

2. Many of the _____ problems will be solved by the subway. (cities)

65

A Flying Gas Station

Read to find out how planes can fill up with fuel in midair.

1   Many military planes are so small that they can't carry much fuel. Some are so big that they use more fuel on one flight than they can take with them at a time. Others are on special missions that require them to fly for many hours without stopping.

2   It wouldn't be very practical for these planes to land every time they needed fuel. Also, there are fewer military air bases than commercial airports. This means a military plane may be far away from an airport when it runs out of fuel.

3   To help solve this problem, there are large planes called aerial refueling tankers that carry enough fuel for these military planes. These tankers refill other planes with fuel in midair.

4   When Charlie was in the U.S. Air Force, he was a pilot on one of these tankers. He always worked with at least three other crew members when he flew a tanker. Charlie and the copilot flew the plane, and the navigator directed the plane's course. The fourth crew member was the boom operator. This person operated the boom, which is a hose that is inside a steel case.

5   When a plane needed fuel, it planned a rendezvous with Charlie's tanker. The two planes would meet at a certain latitude and longitude. When the pilots saw each other's plane, the receiving plane lined up about seventy-five feet below the waiting tanker.

6   The boom operator could see the receiving plane from a window on the bottom of the tanker. At night, lights on the bottom of the tanker help the planes line up. When the planes were in position, the boom operator would "lower the boom," guiding it toward the open fuel tank. The nozzle locked into place while the fuel was being transferred.

7   All this went on high above the earth. All this time, the planes were moving at speeds up to three hundred miles per hour. After ten to twenty minutes, the refueling was complete, and the planes separated. The receiving plane continued on its way, while the tanker returned to its air base.

8   Several times Charlie and his crew had to deal with emergencies. A leak in a plane's fuel tank was one kind of emergency. The leak would make the plane unable to take on enough fuel to get to a base. When the tanker and plane rendezvoused, the boom operator could lock the boom onto one of these crippled planes. The tanker could keep the plane supplied with fuel until it got back to the air base.

9   Charlie has often thought of how nice it would be if the Vista could refuel in the air. It would be a time-saving alternative to landing each time the fuel got low.

Knowing the Words

Write the words from the story that have the meanings below.

1. special operations _____
   (Par. 1)

2. useful _____
   (Par. 2)

3. airplane refueling hose _____
   (Par. 4)

4. meeting _____
   (Par. 5)

5. choice _____
   (Par. 9)

Learning to Study

Look at this map that shows some of the latitudes and longitudes of the Pacific Ocean. Then answer the questions below.

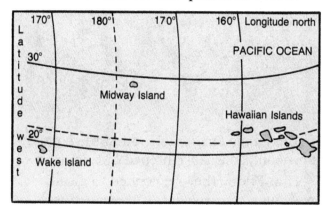

1. If planes rendezvous at 30° north latitude and 180° west longitude, what is the

   closest island? _____

2. What is the latitude and longitude of

   Wake Island? _____

   _____

3. What islands are 22° north latitude and

   157° west longitude? _____

Write the words that these respellings represent.

4. /ron´ di vü/ _____

5. /mil´ ə ter´ ē/ _____

Reading and Thinking

1. Check the most likely conclusions you can make about how long a boom must be.

   _____ It must be three hundred feet long.

   _____ It must be over seventy-five feet long.

   _____ It must be under eighty feet long.

2. Why don't commercial airplanes need to refuel in midair?

   _____

Write **T** before sentences that are true.
Write **F** before those that are false.

3. _____ Four crew members can fly a tanker.

4. _____ All planes must stop to refuel.

5. _____ Tankers can assist crippled planes.

6. _____ All in-air refueling is at night.

7. Check the sentence that best expresses the main idea of this story.

   _____ Crippled planes can be helped back to an air base.

   _____ Tankers have four crew members.

   _____ Planes can be refueled in flight.

8. What is the difference between the job of the pilot and the job of the navigator?

   _____

   _____

Working with Words

The suffix **-er** or **-or** can mean "identity or occupation of." Write the words with **-er** or **-or** that have these meanings.

1. one who navigates _____

2. one who operates _____

3. one who controls _____

Air Rescue

*Read to find out the kind of work that
air-rescue teams do.*

1   Charlie's brother-in-law Sam is a police
officer. He works with the Arizona Highway
Patrol. A few years ago, he became a
paramedic. It had always bothered Sam to
be on the scene of an accident and not know
how to help. When he heard about the air-
rescue division, he knew it would give him
the opportunity he wanted. He applied and
was hired and trained. He's been with the
Flagstaff unit for three years.

2   The wide-open spaces of the Southwest
present special problems for air-rescue
teams. Much of the land is vacant, and
small groups of people are spread out over
large areas.

3   Sam's air-rescue team is an antidote for
these problems. Sam works with another
police officer who is trained as a helicopter
pilot. They are on call to work in a terrain of
deserts, woods, and canyons as well as
populated cities.

4   In a week, the rescue team might fly a
wide variety of missions. One Monday, for
example, Sam's team was sent to aid in the
search for a missing plane. The missing
plane had been flying over a mountainous
area covered with trees. The team was in the
air minutes after getting the message.

5   As they approached the scene, the team
began a carefully organized search. After an
hour they spotted the wreckage. They
landed and located the injured pilot. Sam
treated her for a head injury. A few minutes
later they were on their way to the nearest
hospital, sixty-five miles away.

6   Two days later, the team took part in the
search for a child who had wandered away
from a campsite. During the summer, they
are kept busy with calls like this. In
addition, hikers get hurt, people get swept
off rafts or out of boats and into rivers, and
mountain climbers meet with accidents.

That day they fortunately found the child by
afternoon. He was frightened but not hurt.

7   That Friday they responded to a call
involving a car accident. It happened on a
canyon road. Getting a helicopter in and out
of there took great skill. There were two
victims. Both had severe scrapes and
bruises. Sam administered first aid before
the victims were loaded aboard the
helicopter. Within an hour, the victims were
being admitted to the hospital.

8   On Sunday the rescue team was called
to the scene of a hotel fire. The team
hovered overhead while firefighters tried to
control the fire. It turned out that the fire
was contained in one of the rooms, so Sam
did not have to help rescue anyone.

9   Not all missions have safe endings, but
air-rescue teams have proved their worth
over and over. To those in trouble, the
rescue helicopter is the most beautiful sight
in the world!

68

Knowing the Words

Write the words from the story that have the meanings below.

1. person trained to give first aid _____
   (Par. 1)

2. remedy _____
   (Par. 3)

3. gave or supplied _____
   (Par. 7)

4. stayed in one place in the air _____
   (Par. 8)

In each row below, circle the two words that are related.

5. paramedics   hikers   climbers

6. division   unit   air-rescue

7. wide-open   vacant   populated

8. responded   spotted   located

Learning to Study

A **bibliography** is a list of articles or books that an author referred to when writing. Read these bibliographic entries. Then answer the questions below.

A. **Griffin, Victor.** "Mid-Air Rescue." *Aviation* Vol. 59 (October 1995): 73.

B. **Henderson, Sandra.** *Air Rescue Systems*. New York: Phantom Books, 1992.

1. Check the information given in entry **A** for a magazine article.

   ____ page number   ____ author

   ____ date of magazine   ____ publisher

   ____ name of magazine   ____ article title

2. Check the information given in entry **B** for a book.

   ____ author   ____ page number

   ____ publisher   ____ publishing date

   ____ book title   ____ city of publication

Reading and Thinking

1. Number the events to show the order in which they happened.

   ____ People searched for a missing plane.

   ____ Sam became a paramedic.

   ____ The team went to a car accident.

   ____ The team found a lost child.

   ____ The team went to a hotel fire.

   ____ Sam helped an injured pilot.

2. Check the words that describe a good rescue worker.

   ____ concerned   ____ funny

   ____ quick-thinking   ____ reasonable

Write **F** for fact or **O** for opinion by each statement below.

3. ____ Helicopters are used in air-rescue missions.

4. ____ Air rescue is risky work.

5. ____ Paramedics can give first aid.

6. ____ It takes skill to pilot an air-rescue helicopter.

7. Why are helicopters better for air-rescue work than planes are?

   _____

   _____

Working with Words

The prefix **anti-** means "against." Write the meanings of the words below that have the prefix **anti-**.

1. antigravity _____

2. antifreeze _____

Write the word from the story with the prefix **anti-** that comes from this foreign base word.

3. *didonai,* "to give" _____
   (Par. 3)

The Eye of Radar

Read to find out how radar is used.

1   "Did you know that radar is an acronym and a palindrome?" Pat asked Charlie on a long return flight from Europe.

2   *"A pal in a dome?"* Charlie exclaimed. "What are you talking about?"

3   "I'm talking about the word *radar*," Pat explained. "It's a palindrome because the letters read the same forward and backward like *mom, dad,* and *did.* "It's an acronym because the letters stand for words."

4   "Oh, *radar* stands for *radio detecting and ranging*," Charlie laughed. "I do know that much. I also know that a radar set is made up of a transmitter and a receiver, and without it our jobs would be a lot harder."

5   The transmitter that Charlie mentioned sends out radio waves. When these waves strike something, they bounce off it. Then

they are picked up by the receiving part of the radar set. The speed and intensity of the returning radio waves tell how far away an object is. They also tell if it is moving and at what speed it is moving. Radar waves travel at the speed of light—more than one hundred eighty-six thousand miles per second.

6   Pat and Charlie make good use of radar's ability to identify the weather situation. Often their visibility is dimmed by mist, fog, clouds, or storms. When this happens, they can turn to radar for help. The waves can see areas of heavy rain or snow inside clouds that otherwise look harmless.

7   Instead of looking through storms, radar can also be adjusted to track storms. Weather experts can use radar to see where a storm is and how bad it will get. They can often tell what the storm's path will be.

8   Radar helps planes avoid accidents, too. Radar waves work by hitting objects miles away. These objects are seen as blips of light on a plane's radar screen. Using radar in this way, Pat and Charlie can be warned of danger while it is still distant.

9   For their approach and landing instructions, Pat and Charlie rely on the airport control tower. People in the tower assign each plane a direction and a safe altitude for landing. In the control tower, radar screens show each plane in the vicinity. When visibility is poor, radar can be used to guide the landings.

10   Weather forecasting and flight assistance are not the only uses for radar. Astronomers use it to study other planets. Zoologists use it to study the flight patterns of birds.

11   Ships use radar, too. Radar can pinpoint dangers such as icebergs or rocks.

12   "So, the word *radar* is a palindrome and an acronym," Charlie grinned. "I guess I learn something new every day. How did I ever get along without you, Pat?"

Knowing the Words

Write the words from the story that have the meanings below.

1. finding _____
(Par. 4)

2. covering a distance _____
(Par. 4)

3. strength _____
(Par. 5)

4. ability to see _____
(Par. 6)

5. small dots on radar
screen that show
where objects are _____
(Par. 8)

6. area _____
(Par. 9)

7. people who
study animals _____
(Par. 10)

8. locate precisely _____
(Par. 11)

9. Check the sentence in which *waves* has the same meaning as in paragraph 5.

____ The waves thundered on the beach.

____ Sound travels in waves.

____ The operator waves the all clear.

Learning to Study

Complete this outline of the uses of radar mentioned in paragraphs 6–11.

  I.   Airplane uses

      A. _____

      B. _____

      C. _____

 II.   Scientific Uses

      A. _____

      B. _____

III.   Ship Uses

      A. _____

Reading and Thinking

1. What words does the acronym *radar* represent?

_____

2. What two sections does a radar set have?

_____   _____

3. Light travels faster than sound. Check the statement below that proves this.

____ After lightning is seen, thunder is heard.

____ Sounds are louder on a foggy day.

4. Write the main idea of this story.

_____

Write the word that best completes each sentence.

5. Our _____ was blocked by the thick fog.

   intensity   visibility   acronym

6. The pilot tried to _____ the location of the collision.

   enforce   assist   pinpoint

Working with Words

Rewrite each phrase below. Use possessive forms.

1. the eyes of the pilots

_____

2. the radar screen of the tower

_____

3. a tool of forecasters

_____

4. the instructions of the control tower

_____

71

Air Traffic Control

Read to find out how important the work of air traffic control is.

1   "Even if you are thirty-one, your mom and I are worried about you, Pat. Every time we hear about a collision, we get frantic," Pat's father was telling her over the telephone.

2   "I don't worry about it, Dad. Every day four hundred planes take off or land safely at this airport alone," Pat explained. "Besides, it's not chaos. We have strict regulations. Air traffic controllers watch our every move. We don't take off or land without them. We don't even change altitude or direction without permission from air traffic control.

3   "In the air, each plane appears as a blip on a controller's radar screen," Pat continued. "A controller's job is to regulate the movements of planes on each level of air space. Controllers make sure safe distances are maintained between aircraft. If planes come within five hundred vertical feet of each other, the planes are alerted."

4   "Those are called near misses, right?" Pat's father said. "I read about some of those. Now do you see why your mom and I worry?"

5   "Yes, but there are a lot of reasons flying is safe. For one thing, the new radar screens have automatic snitch alarms. Planes move across a controller's screen in the middle of a circle. If two circles from two planes intersect, an alarm sounds. The controller is alerted that the planes are closer than five horizontal miles apart," Pat explained.

6   "Yes, but at the speeds you fly, two planes five miles apart that are headed toward each other could crash in a few seconds," Pat's father added.

7   "I know," Pat said. "Many planes have traffic alert and collision avoidance systems, too. Those systems automatically alert the pilots to a risk of collision.

8   "Pretty soon, we will be able to program computers with our flight plans and weather data. That will give the controllers more time to watch for emergencies," Pat added.

9   "All I know is that I breathe a sigh of relief when I know you're safely on the ground," her father concluded.

10   "All I know is that if I don't leave now, I'll be late for work," Pat replied. "I'll call you when we get to Quebec." With that, Pat hung up, grabbed her suitcase, and raced out to the Vista. Charlie was just completing the preflight check.

11   Soon they were ready for takeoff. Pat said over the radio, "Columbus, Vista, November nine eight five seven Victor. Ready to go runway two eight left, over."

12   "Vista, five seven Victor, clear for takeoff, left turn on course approved," the controller answered.

13   "Vista, five seven Victor," Pat said. With that, Pat and Charlie began to roll down runway twenty-eight. "I'm glad those people are up there," Pat told Charlie as she nodded toward the control tower. "So is my dad!"

Knowing the Words

Write the words from the story that have the meanings below.

1. up and down _____ (Par. 3)

2. inform _____ (Par. 5)

3. cross each other _____ (Par. 5)

4. parallel to the ground _____ (Par. 5)

In each row below, circle the two words that are related.

5. frantic   chaos   relief

6. approved   alerted   alarmed

7. horizontal   automatic   vertical

8. Check the sentence in which *program* has the same meaning as in paragraph 8.

____ Did you see that TV program?

____ I have the program from the game.

____ Program the robot to make lunch.

Working with Words

Add **-ly** to the words in parentheses to complete each sentence below. Change the spelling of the base word if necessary.

1. The plane arrived _____. (safe)

2. The regulations were _____ enforced. (strict)

3. The parachute opened _____. (automatic)

4. They want to be _____ fair with each other. (complete)

Write the compound words from the story that have these meanings.

5. not having _____ (Par. 2)

6. bag to carry clothes _____ (Par. 10)

Reading and Thinking

1. Write a sentence that summarizes what air traffic controllers do.

_____

_____

2. Do you think flying will be more safe or less safe in the future? Explain.

_____

3. Check the most likely reason the author had for writing this story.

____ to explain what air traffic controllers do

____ to tell why Pat's parents worry

____ to explain how safety equipment works

Learning to Study

The communication between pilot and controller is not hard to figure out if you know what the words mean.

In paragraph 11, Pat calls the Columbus control tower. She then identifies her plane, Vista, and the aircraft number N9857V. The words *November* and *Victor* stand for aircraft call letters *N* and *V*. Pat ends her message with the word *over*, which means she is waiting for a response.

Read this radio message and then answer the questions below.

"Boston Tower Control, Vista Echo two four Mike. Permission to land, over."

1. What airport is the pilot calling?

_____

2. What are the call letters and numbers of the plane? _____

3. What does the pilot want? _____

Leave It to the Experts

Read to find out how the weather experts help pilots.

1   Pat and Charlie flew to Quebec, Canada, from Ohio in September. They flew through, above, and around some storms and strong winds. Their flight plan had been altered to miss the bad weather. The alterations were made because of information provided by Dana Philips. She is an airport meteorologist.

2   Weather conditions must be studied constantly at an airport. The weather conditions determine if a plane will take off or be grounded. For this reason, large airports have people such as Dana on duty twenty-four hours a day.

3   Before takeoff, Pat and Charlie filled out their flight plan. Then they checked with Dana to find out what the weather conditions would be during their flight.

4   Dana checks the local weather reports often. A computer puts together a lot of information quickly for Dana to study. Visibility and temperature are checked frequently. Dana also keeps an eye on the Doppler radar to watch for strong or changing winds. She also receives weather reports from other weather stations and from planes in flight.

5   Weather is a very important factor in flying. Strong winds not only can drive a plane far off course, but they can lift it or pull it down if the pilot is not prepared. Winds blowing straight back against a plane can slow it down, forcing it to use more fuel, while winds pushing a plane from the rear help to save fuel.

6   Snow and rain often lower a pilot's visibility, and hail may dent the body or wings of the aircraft. The weight of ice may make a plane much harder to handle. Fog can almost blind a pilot during takeoff or landing. Planes can be struck by lightning, too, but seldom with damaging results.

7   If bad weather is encountered, planes may be grounded until conditions improve. Planes in flight are advised to change course or to land somewhere else.

8   Pilots depend on the meteorologists and news from the weather station. Without the information that Dana gave them, Pat and Charlie could have been in real trouble. Because their flight plan was changed, they flew above most of the bad weather. They also knew they would have a safe landing in Quebec. They were told that although it would be colder there, it would be clear and dry. When they landed, they found out that Dana had been right.

Knowing the Words

Write the words from the story that have the meanings below.

1. changes _____
(Par. 1)

2. weather scientist _____
(Par. 1)

3. always _____
(Par. 2)

4. part of a whole _____
(Par. 5)

5. met by chance _____
(Par. 7)

Write the words from the story that are represented by these abbreviations.

6. Can. _____
(Par. 1)

7. OH _____
(Par. 1)

8. Sept. _____
(Par. 1)

9. hrs. _____
(Par. 2)

10. inf. _____
(Par. 4)

11. wt. _____
(Par. 6)

Working with Words

Add **-er, -ly,** or **-y** to each word below. Then write the best word to complete each sentence.

constant   storm   hard   unexpected   cold

1. We are _____ in search of better weather information.

2. Wind can make a plane _____ to control than if there were no wind.

3. The planes were grounded because the weather was too _____.

4. The weather in Maine was _____ than the weather in Georgia.

5. A wind came up _____ and caused the plane to bounce.

Reading and Thinking

1. Why must weather conditions be watched constantly? _____
_____

2. Check the most likely conclusion you can make after reading this story.

____Meteorologists have training like that of pilots.

____Weather watching is serious business.

____Weather experts use just a few techniques to make decisions.

Write the word that best completes each sentence.

3. We had to wait before taking off until weather _____ improved.

meteorologists   conditions   visibility

4. They had to make _____ in their plans after hearing the report.

alterations   directions   factors

Learning to Study

Read this weather report and then answer the questions below.

> - Partly to mostly cloudy today
> - Highs 24°–30° (F)
> - Cloudy tonight with snow accumulating less than one inch
> - Lows mostly in the 20s
> - Chance of snow 35% tonight
> - Winds west to northwest 15 to 20 mph

1. When might snow fall? _____

2. What is the chance that snow will fall?
_____

3. Will the temperature be above freezing during this time? _____

75

A Cure for the Common Cold

Look for clues that tell you what might happen to Pat and Charlie.

1 It was the kind of day on which you take a coat because you think it's colder than it really is. Pat left her London hotel early to meet Charlie at the airport. Their departure was scheduled for 9:00 A.M. As she took her last ride through London, she noticed a dignified man struggling with an umbrella that had turned inside out. "So long, England," she thought.

2 She met Charlie at 7:00 and found that he had already begun the preflight check. By 8:30, the Vista had been loaded, and they were ready to go. They checked with ground control tower for a final weather report and waited for permission to taxi.

3 At 8:45 they were told that because of low visibility all planes would be grounded until further notice. Although they knew taking off could be dangerous, Pat and Charlie felt this delay was an annoyance since they would have to make up the time in flight.

4 Charlie was eager to leave and return home. He thought he was catching a cold. He wanted to take a hot bath, drink some tea with lemon, and climb into his own bed. At 10:30, they taxied onto the runway.

5 At last their takeoff was approved, and the Vista started slowly down the runway

and then picked up speed. Faster and faster it went until lift overcame gravity, and the plane's nose rose off the pavement.

6 Suddenly there was a jolt as if a huge hand had slapped the plane back to earth. Pat and Charlie both gasped and bounced violently in their seats. The huge plane was racing uncontrollably down a wet runway whose end was fast approaching.

7 Pat's and Charlie's hearts were racing, too, but they kept their heads. They did everything they could to control the plane that had become a mad dog. "Hang on!" Charlie shouted as they hit the marsh at the end of the runway. After several more thuds, they came to a stop.

8 Both pilots were stunned. For a minute neither spoke, and then at the same time they said, "What happened?"

9 "Vista, nine eight five seven!" the controller shouted. "Are you OK?"

10 "London, this is Vista 57 Victor. Why didn't you tell us this was a roller coaster?" Charlie answered as he quickly regained his sense of humor.

11 In the next minute, an ambulance and fire engine appeared from nowhere. Under protest, Pat and Charlie were taken to a nearby hospital to make sure neither had been injured.

12 After getting a clean bill of health from the hospital and discovering that their plane was still in one piece, Pat and Charlie decided to get a bite to eat. "I'm sure they'll decide that was a low-altitude wind shear that we encountered," Pat said.

13 "For sure," Charlie agreed. "I had no idea this would be such an exciting trip. There is, however, one excellent result."

14 "Is it that we'll be able to remain in London a few more days until they dig our plane out of the mud?" asked Pat.

15 "No!" said Charlie. "I had such a shock that my cold is gone!"

Knowing the Words

Write the words from the story that have the meanings below.

1. noble _____
   (Par. 1)

2. bother _____
   (Par. 3)

3. roughly and strongly _____
   (Par. 6)

4. got back _____
   (Par. 10)

5. severe wind caused
   by a violent thunderstorm _____
   (Par. 12)

Write the words from the story that are synonyms (words that have the same or nearly the same meaning) for these words.

6. postponement _____
   (Par. 3)

7. dazed _____
   (Par. 8)

8. objection _____
   (Par. 11)

In each row below, circle the three words that are related.

9. jolt   bounce   thud   race

10. departure   leave   pre-flight   takeoff

11. Check the correct meaning of the metaphor, *the plane that had become a mad dog*, from paragraph 7.

    _____ The plane turned into a wild dog.

    _____ The plane was out of control.

Working with Words

Write the open or closed compound words from the story that are formed by adding words to these words.

1. came _____
   (Par. 5)

2. coaster _____
   (Par. 10)

3. where _____
   (Par. 11)

4. shear _____
   (Par. 12)

Reading and Thinking

1. Check the most likely reason the author had for writing this story.

   _____ to entertain

   _____ to persuade

2. Check the word that best describes the mood of this story.

   _____ suspenseful   _____ serious

   _____ humorous   _____ romantic

3. Check the things that show that Pat and Charlie were frightened.

   _____ Their hearts were racing.

   _____ Charlie was catching a bad cold.

   _____ They were annoyed with the delay.

   _____ They gasped in unison.

4. Check the words below that describe the flying weather in this story.

   _____ stormy   _____ sunny

   _____ rainy   _____ windy

   _____ hot   _____ cold

Learning to Study

Study this weather table for the first days of March, and then answer the questions below.

March Sun Data			Temperature Extremes			
Date	Sunrise	Sunset	High	Year	Low	Year
1	7:05	6:23	65	1972	-2	1967
2	7:04	6:24	70	1976	0	1980
3	7:02	6:25	75	1974	0	1943
4	7:01	6:26	78	1946	-1	1943

1. Are the days getting shorter or longer?

   _____

2. In what year was the temperature

   coldest on March 3? _____

3. When is sunset on March 2? _____

Over the Bermuda Triangle

Read to see what makes the Bermuda Triangle so mysterious.

1   Pat and Charlie were flying a cargo of frozen foods on a course from Miami to Bermuda. As the plane fought a rough wind current, Pat scanned the choppy Atlantic far below. "I have to tell you," she said, "this place is pretty spooky."

2   "You mean to tell me you're frightened, Pat? Just because more than fifty planes and ships have disappeared in this area without a trace shouldn't be any cause for alarm," Charlie said laughing.

3   "It's not funny!" Pat said. "Nothing about it makes sense. This area is called the Bermuda Triangle, but it has four sides. It starts at Bermuda and extends to southern Virginia. Then it goes down to the tip of Florida, across to Puerto Rico, and back to Bermuda."

4   "It doesn't shape up, whatever it is," said Charlie with a straight face. "The first recorded disappearance happened in the mid-nineteenth century, didn't it?"

5   "I think so," said Pat. "In some instances ships were found, but there was no trace of the crew or passengers. Some ships and planes have been lost completely."

6   "Yes, and it has happened in spite of radio and modern equipment, too," said Charlie. "Many have vanished in fair weather, right out of the blue."

7   "That's right. There were those five navy bombers that disappeared in 1945," Pat added. "They radioed that they were lost right before they vanished."

8   "The plane that was sent to rescue them vanished, also," Charlie said.

9   "There was that occurrence in 1968 when a submarine vanished, too," Pat continued. "It was discovered on the ocean floor several months later, but no one could explain what had happened to it."

10   "Now you're giving me the creeps," Charlie said. "It is weird, but there could be any number of answers to the riddle. The Gulf Stream could be partly to blame. It behaves in unpredictable ways. There's also that strange flow of high-altitude wind that sweeps in without warning."

11   "You're right," Pat agreed. "Heavy storms could throw compasses off, too. Navigators could lose track of their position, and if that happened, the planes could run out of fuel."

12   Charlie frowned and said, "But most people think that the answer is yet to be discovered."

13   "Well, whatever the explanation, this pilot refuses to be jinxed," Pat said firmly. "Most planes make it through just fine, and so will we."

14   "Let's think about something else," said Charlie. "How about some lunch?"

15   Pat smiled as Charlie handed her a lunch bag. "Oh, good, it's a ham sandwich with pickle and mustard," she said.

16   "It also has Bermuda onion!" added Charlie. "I'll make it disappear in no time."

Knowing the Words

Write the words from the story that have the meanings below.

1. quickly looked over _____
(Par. 1)

2. rough _____
(Par. 1)

3. examples or cases _____
(Par. 5)

4. a happening _____
(Par. 9)

5. not certain _____
(Par. 10)

In each row below, circle the two words that are related.

6. disappeared   vanished   abandoned

7. discovered   mysterious   weird

8. Check the sentence in which *course* has the same meaning as in paragraph 1.

_____ Of course we will go with you.

_____ What math course should I take?

_____ That course will get us there.

Working with Words

Add a prefix or a suffix from the list below to each word to form a new word. You may have to change the spelling of the base word before adding a suffix.

| dis-   -ly   -y   -able |

1. firm

_____

2. mysterious

_____

3. predict

_____

4. cover

_____

5. chop

_____

6. appear

_____

7. creep

_____

8. complete

_____

9. explain

_____

10. spook

_____

Reading and Thinking

Write **F** for fact or **O** for opinion before each statement below.

1. _____ Five bombers disappeared in 1945.

2. _____ Storms caused the disappearances.

3. _____ The Bermuda Triangle is a mysterious place.

4. _____ Navigation instruments can be affected by the weather.

5. Check the sequence that shows how Charlie's attitude about the Bermuda Triangle changed throughout the story.

_____ from humorous to serious to humorous

_____ from serious to humorous to serious

_____ from mysterious to humorous to serious

Learning to Study

Look at this map, and then answer the questions below.

1. Based on Pat's description in paragraph 3, draw lines around the area called the Bermuda Triangle.

2. What group of islands lies within the

Bermuda Triangle? _____

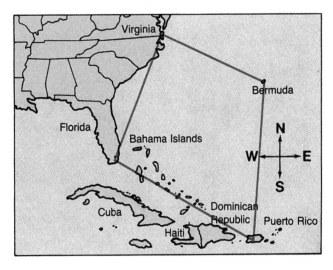

Unidentified Flying Objects

Read to find out if Pat and Charlie believe unidentified flying objects exist.

1   "Charlie," asked Pat as they were on their way back from Bermuda, "have you ever seen a UFO?"

2   "An unidentified flying object?" Charlie said. "No, I can't say that I have. At least if I saw one, I didn't know that I saw one. Why, is there something you're not telling me?"

3   "No," Pat answered, "I was just curious. Do you believe they exist?"

4   "Well, I think lots of things are possible, Pat. Why are you curious?" Charlie asked.

5   "Well, a friend of mine asked me if I believed UFOs existed. She said she had seen some unusual lights in the sky. She wondered what I thought about them. You know, in 1938 when radio broadcasted a fictional account of a Martian landing in New Jersey, there was mass hysteria," Pat said.

6   "All I know is that the Air Force takes UFOs seriously. They investigated more than fifteen thousand reports of sightings. They also sponsored a study by scientists over a two-year period. The scientists found logical explanations for most of the reports. Lots of the things were explained as meteors, rockets, stars, weather balloons, or other types of aircraft," Charlie said.

7   "They couldn't account for all of them, could they?" said Pat.

8   "No," said Charlie. "However, they did not find any evidence that the UFOs came from other planets, either. In the end, they concluded that no matter what, UFOs were not a threat to national security."

9   "Is the Air Force still studying them?" asked Pat.

10   "Not officially, but I do know that other groups are. You know, Pat, the more publicity there is about UFOs, the more sightings there are," Charlie said.

11   "So you don't believe that most people see what they think they see," Pat smiled.

12   "I think people do see some odd things. There have been some reliable, well-documented sightings, though," Charlie said. "For example, I heard about an instance in the 50s when a UFO was tracked on radar in England. Two stations detected several objects moving at high speeds. At the same time, two tower operators and a pilot saw a bright light passing overhead."

13   Charlie continued, "A plane was sent up to make airborne radar contact, but the object moved behind the plane. Then all radar contact was lost. I think that was the most puzzling of all the cases."

14   "Well, it's beyond my imagination," Pat said. "I guess I just don't often think about things I don't understand. I believe anything is possible."

15   "The universe is a big place," Charlie said. "We can't possibly understand even a fraction of it. Anyway, I don't think I really want to know if UFOs exist. There's already too much I can't figure out."

Knowing the Words

Write the words from the story that have the meanings below.

1. to be real
   or alive _____
   (Par. 3)

2. story _____
   (Par. 5)

3. great excitement _____
   (Par. 5)

4. sensible _____
   (Par. 6)

5. shooting stars _____
   (Par. 6)

Drop the prefix from each word below to write the words that are antonyms (words that mean the opposite).

6. unidentified _____

7. illogical _____

8. insecurity _____

9. unreliable _____

10. Write a **7** before the sentence in which *account* has the same meaning as in paragraph 7. Write a **5** before the sentence in which *account* has the same meaning as in paragraph 5.

   _____ We gave the full account.

   _____ We could not account for the missing money.

Working with Words

Rewrite each phrase below. Use possessive forms.

1. the explanation of Charlie

   _____

2. the explanation of the scientist

   _____

3. the explanations of the scientists

   _____

Reading and Thinking

1. Check the phrase that best expresses the main idea of this story.

   _____ a radio broadcast

   _____ a discussion of UFOs

   _____ a scientist's study

2. Why was there mass hysteria in 1938 after a radio broadcast?

   _____

Write the word that best completes each sentence.

3. They saw some _____ of a crime.

   philosophy   evidence   security

4. They _____ the report.

   unidentified   investigated   frightened

Learning to Study

1. Check each reference you might use to find out more on UFOs.

   _____ encyclopedia   _____ dictionary

   _____ card catalog   _____ almanac

   _____ *Readers' Guide*   _____ atlas

Read these outline headings for a story on UFOs and answer the questions below.

   I.   Daytime sightings
   II. Fictional accounts
   III. Radar sightings

2. Which item does not belong in the story?

   _____

3. Check the items that could be included in this story.

   _____ face-to-face encounters

   _____ nighttime sightings

   _____ the Bermuda Triangle

The Golden Age of Flight

Read to find out about the accomplishments of African-American pilots.

1   The next time Pat and Charlie were in Washington, D.C., they met Pat's friend Charlotte. She took them to an aviation museum.

2   The first thing they saw was an exhibit on African-American aviators from the golden age of aviation. The achievements of Bessie Coleman caught their eyes at once.

3   Bessie Coleman had been born in Texas in 1893. She decided to become a pilot. She found, though, that she had to go to France for her flying lessons. At the time, African Americans were not allowed in flying school. At twenty-nine she became the first African-American female pilot in the United States to have a flying license. But four years later at an air show, her plane went out of control and crashed. In spite of her flying skills, she met a premature death.

4   Coleman's life had been an inspiration to many people who wanted to fly. Many African Americans, however, found that they were denied flying lessons. Because of this, William J. Powell, an engineer, established the Bessie Coleman Aeroclub in California. There, African Americans were encouraged to take to the air.

5   Two years after the club opened, it sponsored an air show that featured six pilots. James Herman Banning, chief pilot and instructor at the Coleman school, was one of the daredevils.

6   Banning had always dreamed of flying and was mechanically inclined. In 1924 in Iowa he had learned how to fly. He then went west and taught at the Coleman School. His ambition was to set a flight record.

7   On September 18, 1932, he and his mechanic took off on a transcontinental flight. They became known as the *Flying*

Hobos. They left California with only one hundred dollars. They had to depend upon people in the towns where they landed for food and shelter. By the time they reached Eagle Rock, Long Island, on October 9, they were heroes.

8   The Coleman school was not the only place for African-American aviators. Pat, Charlotte, and Charlie learned that Chicago, too, was a center for African-American pilots during the golden age of flight. There, Willie "Suicide" Jones broke a parachute jumping record. Other Chicago aviators, such as Willa Brown, worked to publicize the achievements of African-American pilots.

9   One of these pilots was Cornelius Coffey. He had gone on his first plane ride in 1919 and was bitten by the flying bug. He soon transferred his knowledge of auto mechanics to planes. This was easy to do because most planes used converted car engines. After a long career in aviation, Coffey met Colonel Guy Buford, America's first African-American astronaut.

10   "It's just like Lindbergh!" Charlotte said. "Coffey's life spanned the history of flight, too. If it weren't for fearless people like them, we might not be flying today."

Knowing the Words

Write the words from the story that have the meanings below.

1. before the usual time _____
   (Par. 3)

2. an influence _____
   (Par. 4)

3. interested in _____
   (Par. 6)

4. changed from
   one to the other _____
   (Par. 9)

5. Check the correct meaning of the idiom *caught their eyes* from paragraph 2.

   ____ grabbed their eyeballs

   ____ got their attention

6. Check the correct meaning of the idiom *bitten by the flying bug* in paragraph 9.

   ____ really wanted to fly

   ____ bitten by a flying insect

Working with Words

Write the words from the story that have the given prefixes and that come from these foreign base words.

1. **in-** + *spirare*
   meaning "to breathe" _____
   (Par. 4)

2. **en-** + *corage*,
   meaning "courage" _____
   (Par. 4)

3. **in-** + *struere*,
   meaning "to build" _____
   (Par. 5)

4. **in-** + *clinare*,
   meaning "to lean" _____
   (Par. 6)

Write the words from the story that have the suffix **-ly** and that are formed from these base words.

5. mechanical _____

6. short _____

Reading and Thinking

1. Why did William J. Powell establish a flight school?

   _____

Write **C** before statements that describe Cornelius Coffey. Write **L** before statements that describe Charles Lindbergh in the story on page 32. Write **C/L** before statements that describe both.

2. ____ He got a lot of publicity.

3. ____ His life spanned flight history.

4. ____ He was mechanically inclined.

Write **T** before the statements that are true. Write **F** before those that are false.

5. ____ African-American women never became pilots.

6. ____ In 1932, James Banning made a transcontinental flight.

7. ____ Many African Americans wanted to fly planes.

8. ____ Until 1964, African-Americans had to go to France to get flying lessons.

Learning to Study

Complete this partial outline of African-American aviators and their accomplishments.

  I. Bessie Coleman

     A. _____

         _____

     B. _____

 II. William J. Powell

     A. _____

     B. _____

III. James Herman Banning

     A. _____

     B. _____

Yesterday, Today, Tomorrow

Read to see how Pat's past may become her future.

1 The exhibit in the Air and Space Museum was breathtaking. Without exception, it was the best aviation exhibit Pat, Charlie, and Charlotte had ever seen. It had some authentic aircraft from the old days. Hanging from the ceiling was the Wright brothers' *Flyer*. Behind it was Charles Lindbergh's *Spirit of St. Louis*. Nearby was the first aircraft to break the sound barrier. Beneath the *Flyer* was the *Apollo 11*, which had made a trip to the moon.

2 The three friends found that there wasn't time to see the rest of the exhibits. They agreed to find their own favorites and meet at closing time. Charlie went to see the space exhibit. Charlotte headed toward the experimental aircraft. Pat decided to look at historical aircraft.

3 In one room, Pat saw open-cockpit mail planes that pilots once flew from town to town. At times, these adventurous pilots were guided only by looking for familiar landmarks on the ground.

4 In the next room, Pat saw the *Winnie Mae*, the plane that Wiley Post flew around the world. There were also exhibits about Amelia Earhart, Jacqueline Cochran, and other famous pilots.

5 When Pat entered another room, she found some balloons that were two hundred years old. They had carried some of the first daring aeronauts. As she took a closer look at the balloons, she thought she heard a voice from out of her own past calling her name. Turning around, she found herself looking at her college boyfriend, Ross. She hadn't seen him for over ten years.

6 "Ross, I can't believe it's you!" she exclaimed, not sure if she was dreaming.

7 "What are you doing here?" he asked.

8 "I'm visiting a friend for the weekend, but what about you?" Pat asked.

9 "Oh, I work here. I put these exhibits together," Ross explained.

10 "You're in aviation, too? I was a flight instructor for a while, and now I'm a cargo pilot," she said.

11 "I'm not surprised," Ross chuckled. "You always loved flying. Hey, what are you doing after you leave here?"

12 "My friends and I are planning to go out to dinner," replied Pat. "I'd like to introduce you to them if you have the evening free."

13 I'd be delighted!" Ross responded.

14 The two made plans to meet when the museum closed. Then Ross returned to work. Pat continued walking through the exhibit, but now she was walking on air. At 5:00, Pat introduced Ross to Charlotte and Charlie as they headed to the restaurant.

15 After dinner, Charlotte asked the question that Pat was afraid to ask, "Are you married, Ross?"

16 "No," Ross answered with a shy smile, "I never found anybody like Pat."

17 "Pat's not married either," Charlie explained as Pat's face turned a bright red. "She'll be here again next week."

18 "We'll have to get together," Ross said.

19 And they did.

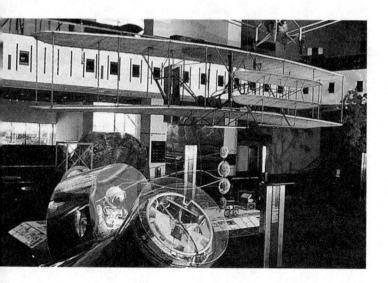

Knowing the Words

Write the words from the story that have the meanings below.

1. something left out _____
   (Par. 1)

2. genuine _____
   (Par. 1)

3. objects used as guides _____
   (Par. 3)

4. balloon or airship fliers _____
   (Par. 5)

5. Check the sentence in which *past* has the same meaning as in paragraph 5.

   ____ I could not see past the trees.

   ____ In the past twenty minutes, the phone has rung six times.

   ____ In the past, we would not have found the error.

Write the words from the story that are antonyms (words that mean the opposite) of these words.

6. floor _____
   (Par. 1)

7. above _____
   (Par. 1)

8. unfamiliar _____
   (Par. 3)

9. apart _____
   (Par. 9)

10. dull _____
    (Par. 17)

Working with Words

Write the compound words from the story that are formed by adding to these words.

1. taking _____
   (Par. 1)

2. open _____
   (Par. 3)

3. marks _____
   (Par. 3)

4. end _____
   (Par. 8)

Reading and Thinking

1. Check the phrase that best expresses the main idea of this story.

   ____ famous planes

   ____ Pat's friends

   ____ the past, present, and future

2. Check the most likely conclusion you can make about the navigation system of the open-cockpit mail planes.

   ____ There were few instruments.

   ____ They had radio-controlled systems.

   ____ They used radar for navigation.

3. Check the conclusions you can make based on the fact that Pat was "walking on air" after she saw Ross.

   ____ She was pleased to see Ross.

   ____ She was enjoying the exhibit.

   ____ She had lost a lot of weight.

   ____ Her feet were sore.

   ____ She was happy that Ross wanted to go to dinner with her.

4. Do you think Pat and Ross will continue to see each other? Explain.

   _____

   _____

Learning to Study

Read this dictionary entry. Then write the parts of the entry that are requested below.

break / brāk / *vb* **broke; bro ken 1** to suddenly separate; SHATTER, CUT **2** to fail to keep **3** to crush

1. entry word _____

2. part of speech abbreviation _____

3. irregular forms _____

4. respelling _____

Checking Understanding

Test 1   These exercises are to be completed after reading the story on page 10.

1. Check two sentences that are true. (2)

_____ Pterodactyls were large birds.

_____ Pterodactyl fossils have been found.

_____ Pat and Charlie were heading north in their plane.

2. National Airport is in _____.

3. Check another good title for this story.

_____ Fossils of West Texas

_____ Prehistoric Animals

_____ A Model of a Flying Reptile

4. Why was the model tested?

_____

Number of Words
Read per Minute [ ]

5. Pterodactyls lived in _____ times.

6. How were the model's wings powered?

_____

7. Number these events in the order in which they happen in the story.

_____ Pat called the control tower.

_____ Charlie saw the reptile.

_____ Frank told them about the model.

_____ Charlie made a joke about birds.

_____ Pat said she had been startled.

_____ Pat saw the reptile below them.

8. Write two things these reptiles did to fly. (2) _____

Test Score
(Possible Score—10) [ ]

Test 2   These exercises are to be completed after reading the story on page 30.

1. Check another good title for this story.

_____ Overnight Fame

_____ An Extraordinary Person

_____ Around the World

2. Becoming a pilot was hard for Earhart because _____.

3. Earhart felt she did not deserve overnight fame because _____

_____.

4. Write two records that Earhart set. (2)

_____

_____

Number of Words
Read per Minute [ ]

5. Check two sentences that are true. (2)

_____ Earhart had average flying skills.

_____ Earhart flew around the world.

_____ Earhart was calm under pressure.

_____ Earhart wasn't immediately accepted by other pilots.

6. Fred Noonan was Earhart's _____.

7. Write one possible reason for Earhart's disappearance. _____

_____

8. Why is Earhart's story a mystery?

_____

Test Score
(Possible Score—10) [ ]

86

Checking Understanding

Test 3   These exercises are to be completed after reading the story on page 44.

1. Number these events in the order in which they happened in the story.

   _____ Jane explained hang gliders.

   _____ Charlotte joked about Pat's fear.

   _____ Jane took off in her hang glider.

   _____ Charlotte persuaded Pat to learn about hang gliding.

   _____ Pat saw a young girl and an older man try hang gliding.

   _____ Pat agreed to try hang gliding.

2. Check two sentences that are true. (2)

   _____ Pat had not flown in a sailplane.

   _____ A hang glider is triangular.

   _____ A new kind of airfoil was patented in the 1950s.

   _____ Pat was fond of hang gliding.

3. Write two things that should be worn to be safe while hang gliding. (2)

   _____

4. Check another good title for the story.

   _____ The Wind Is Our Friend

   _____ Pat's Hang Gliding Lesson

   _____ An Afternoon in Virginia

5. Many people began hang gliding after

   _____ .

6. Hang gliders are steered by _____ .

7. Jane _____ hang gliding.

   _____ fears   _____ dislikes   _____ enjoys

8. Hang gliders become airborne when

   _____ .

Number of Words Read per Minute [ ]

Test Score (Possible Score–10) [ ]

Test 4   These exercises are to be completed after reading the story on page 78.

1. In what ocean is the Bermuda Triangle? _____

2. Why is the Bermuda Triangle weird?

   _____

3. Write two reasons why planes vanish in the Bermuda Triangle. (2)

   _____

4. Pat refused to be _____ .

   _____ hungry   _____ calm   _____ jinxed

5. Planes could run out of fuel in storms

   because _____ .

6. Check two sentences that are true. (2)

   _____ The Bermuda Triangle has four sides.

   _____ All planes vanish in the Triangle.

   _____ More than fifty planes and ships have been lost in the Triangle.

7. Check another good title for this story.

   _____ Mystery in the Atlantic Ocean

   _____ Bermuda Onion for Lunch

   _____ Frozen Foods for Bermuda

8. The Gulf Stream could cause trouble

   because _____ .

Number of Words Read per Minute [ ]

Test Score (Possible Score–10) [ ]

Knowing the Words

Write the words from the story that have the meanings below.

1. assistant pilot _____copilot_____ (Par. 2)
2. teacher _____instructor_____ (Par. 2)
3. decide before knowing the facts _____prejudge_____ (Par. 4)
4. one who schedules airplane flights _____dispatcher_____ (Par. 5)
5. next to _____adjoining_____ (Par. 6)
6. unaware _____unconsciously_____ (Par. 10)
7. airplane body _____fuselage_____ (Par. 11)
8. area where the pilot sits _____cockpit_____ (Par. 13)

An **idiom** is a phrase that cannot be understood by the meaning of its words. The phrase *break the ice* is an idiom. It means "to start a conversation." Find the phrases that are idioms in the story and write them.

9. _____a whale of a job_____ (Par. 2)
10. _____learn the ropes_____ (Par. 18)

Learning to Study

Dictionary entry words appear in dark print and are divided by spaces. These spaces show where the words can be divided at the end of a line of writing. Write the words below in syllables and in alphabetical order as they would appear as entries.

copilot	fuselage	instructor
cockpit	prejudge	dispatcher

1. cock pit   4. fu se lage
2. co pi lot   5. in struc tor
3. dis patch er   6. pre judge

Reading and Thinking

1. Check each word or phrase that describes Charlie in the story.
   - ✓ excitable
   - ✓ respects Pat
   - ___ shy

2. Check each word or phrase that describes Pat in this story.
   - ✓ capable
   - ___ athletic
   - ✓ loves flying

3. Check the most likely outcome of this story.
   - ___ Pat will resent Charlie.
   - ✓ Pat and Charlie will get along.
   - ___ Charlie will resent Pat.

Working with Words

A **suffix** is a letter or group of letters added to the end of a word to change the word's meaning or part of speech. The suffix **-ly** usually means "in a certain way." Write the words from the story that have the suffix **-ly** and that are formed from these base words.

1. real _____really_____ (Par. 2)
2. sudden _____suddenly_____ (Par. 5)
3. unconscious _____unconsciously_____ (Par. 10)
4. gentle _____gently_____ (Par. 11)
5. amaze _____amazingly_____ (Par. 11)
6. smooth _____smoothly_____ (Par. 11)
7. certain _____certainly_____ (Par. 19)
8. like _____likely_____ (Par. 20)
9. ashamed _____ashamedly_____ (Par. 20)

Knowing the Words

Write the words from the story that have the meanings below.

1. baggage _____luggage_____ (Par. 4)
2. head _____helm_____ (Par. 5)
3. dangerous _____hazardous_____ (Par. 6)
4. prompt _____punctual_____ (Par. 8)
5. buyers _____consumers_____ (Par. 10)
6. carried _____transported_____ (Par. 11)

7. Find the **idiom** in the story and write it on the first line. Write the meaning of the idiom on the second line.

   _____a lot of water under the bridge_____ (Par. 2)

   _____a lot of time has gone by_____
   (Answers may vary.)

Learning to Study

Dictionary definitions, or meanings, are most often short phrases, but they can also be single words. Find the entry words below in a dictionary. Then write the definitions that relate to air travel. (Answers may vary.)

1. taxi _____travel slowly on the ground_____

2. runway _____paved airport landing strip_____

3. cargo _____load of goods carried by airplane_____

4. container _____box used to hold something_____

5. bay _____section of an airplane_____

Reading and Thinking

1. Check the word that best describes Pa[t] when she says, "We haven't always bee[n] punctual."
   - ___ lazy
   - ✓ honest
   - ___ early

2. Check the sentence that best expresse[s] the main idea of this story.
   - ___ A snake was lost in flight.
   - ___ Pat and Charlie are friends.
   - ✓ Cargo planes ship a variety of goods.

3. Based on what you read in this story, check the words that describe the Vista[.]
   - ✓ huge   ___ modern
   - ✓ fast   ✓ dark inside

Write the word that best completes each sentence.

4. The control tower is _____adjoining_____ the hangar.

   connecting   adjoining   transport[ing]

5. The _____fuselage_____ is the body o[f] an airplane.

   fuselage   cockpit   hangar

Working with Words

A **prefix** is a letter or a group of letters added to the beginning of a word to change its meaning. The prefix **mis-** means "badly" or "wrongly." Add the prefix **mis-** to these words.

1. labeled _____mislabeled_____
2. fortune _____misfortune_____
3. behave _____misbehave_____
4. place _____misplace_____

3

Knowing the Words

Write the words from the story that have the meanings below.

1. transportation station _____terminal_____ (Par. 3)
2. moving carrier _____conveyor_____ (Par. 3)
3. paved area for loading planes _____ramp_____ (Par. 5)
4. sensational _____spectacular_____ (Par. 8)
5. scenery _____landscape_____ (Par. 8)

A **simile** is a figure of speech in which two unlike things are compared. Similes use the word *like* or *as*. Write the actual meaning of the similes from paragraph 8.

6. *landscape was like a toy city*
   _____Everything looked tiny._____

7. *clouds looked like puffs of cotton*
   _____The clouds were white and puffy._____
   (Answers may vary.)

Working with Words

A **compound word** is formed by putting two or more words together to make a new word. Write the compound words from the story that are formed by adding to these words.

1. air _____airport_____ (Par. 2)
2. taxi _____taxiway_____ (Par. 5)
3. stair _____stairway_____ (Par. 5)
4. seat _____seatbelt_____ (Par. 7)
5. off _____takeoff_____ (Par. 7)
6. land _____landscape_____ (Par. 8)
7. sun _____sunlight_____ (Par. 8)
8. run _____runway_____ (Par. 9)

Reading and Thinking

1. Number the events to show the order in which they happened in time.
   - 6 Pat and Charlie were cruising at thirty thousand feet.
   - 2 Pat watched her suitcases on the airport's conveyor belt.
   - 1 Pat packed her suitcases.
   - 4 Pat saw the cockpit.
   - 5 Pat saw her cousin waving.
   - 3 Pat saw her parents wave.

2. Authors write stories to inform, to entertain, or to persuade. Check the most likely reason the author had for writing this story.
   - ✓ to inform
   - ___ to entertain
   - ___ to persuade

3. Why did Pat pack her luggage a month before her trip? _____She was excited about her first plane trip._____
   (Answers may vary.)

Learning to Study

Using this airline flight schedule and information from the story, write the following information about Pat's flight.

Flight Schedule

Flight	Destination	Departing	Arriving	Gate
238	Newark, NJ	9:45 A.M.	1:00 P.M.	15
965	Toronto, ON	1:15 P.M.	5:45 P.M.	17
455	Bangor, ME	3:45 P.M.	7:01 P.M.	5

1. Gate Number _____5_____
2. Flight Number _____455_____
3. Departure Time _____3:45 P.M._____
4. Arrival Time _____7:01 P.M._____
5. Destination _____Bangor, ME_____

Knowing the Words

Write the words from the story that have the meanings below.

1. lever that regulates the flow of fuel to an engine _____throttle_____ (Par. 3)
2. height above the earth _____altitude_____ (Par. 4)
3. parts put together _____assembly_____ (Par. 5)
4. planned movements _____maneuvers_____ (Par. 8)
5. downward movement _____descent_____ (Par. 8)

A **metaphor** is a figure of speech in which two unlike objects are compared directly. Unlike a simile, the word *like* or *as* is not used to make the comparison. Check the correct meaning of the metaphor, *my hands were blocks of ice*, from paragraph 6.

6. ✓ I was nervous.
   ___ My hands had been replaced by large ice cubes.

Check the correct meaning of the metaphor, *my heart became a rocket*, in paragraph 6.

7. ___ My heart turned into a rocket.
   ✓ I was frightened.

Working with Words

The suffix **-y** can mean "full of" or "like." Write the words from the story that have the suffix **-y** and are formed from these base words.

1. scare _____scary_____ (Par. 3)
2. assemble _____assembly_____ (Par. 5)

Write the words that have the suffix **-y** and the meanings below.

3. full of gloom _____gloomy_____
4. full of fun _____funny_____

Reading and Thinking

1. Check the sentence that tells the reaso[n] Charlie was scared in the story.
   - ___ Charlie had never been in an airplane before.
   - ✓ Charlie had not flown solo before.
   - ___ The airplane had not been checke[d]

2. Why do you think Charlie forgot there were other people in the universe?
   _____The plane was quiet, and he was_____ _____concentrating on his first solo flight._____
   (Answers may vary.)

List two facts that lead you to conclude tha[t] Charlie had a good first instructor.

3. _____The instructor made him check everything_____
4. _____He passed his exam with flying colors._____
   (Answers may vary.)

Write the word that best completes each sentence.

5. The first pilots must have been very _____heroic_____.

   quiet   heroic   scary

6. Before Pat starts the engine, she does a[n] _____preflight_____ check.

   beginner's   altitude   preflight

Learning to Study

Many kinds of entry words can be found in most dictionaries. Match the types of entrie[s] with the correct examples.

1. c proper noun   a. -ly
2. d prefix   b. *learn the rope[s]*
3. a suffix   c. Ohio
4. e abbreviation   d. **mis-**
5. b idiom   e. Dr.

7

Knowing the Words

Write the words from the story that have the meanings below.

1. of the time before written history __prehistoric__ (Par. 3)

2. extinct flying reptile __pterodactyl__ (Par. 9)

3. hardened animal or plant remains __fossils__ (Par. 12)

4. large vultures __condors__ (Par. 18)

An **abbreviation** is a short form of a word or group of words. Write the words from the story that are represented by these abbreviations.

5. D.C. __District of Columbia__ (Par. 4)

6. n. __north__ (Par. 6)

7. ft. __foot__ (Par. 9)

8. mus. __museum__ (Par. 11)

9. elec. __electric__ (Par. 11)

10. S.A. __South American__ (Par. 18)

Learning to Study

A **pronunciation key** is a list of sound symbols and key words that tell how to pronounce dictionary entry words. A pronunciation key can be found on the inside back cover of this book. Use this key to write the words that each of these respellings represents.

1. /hŏr´ ə bəl/ __horrible__

2. /fə mil´ yər/ __familiar__

3. /ter´ ə dak´ təl/ __pterodactyl__

4. /mŏd´ əl/ __model__

5. /myū zē´ əm/ __museum__

Reading and Thinking

A **fact** is something that is known to be true. An **opinion** is what a person believes. An opinion may or may not be true. Write **F** for fact or **O** for opinion before each statement below.

1. _O_ The hawk is a huge bird.

2. _O_ The pterodactyl was scary.

3. _F_ The Smithsonian Institution is in Washington, D.C.

4. _F_ A condor's wingspread is nine feet.

Write **T** before statements that are true. Write **F** before those that are false.

5. _T_ Pterodactyls were reptiles that are believed to have flown.

6. _T_ The White House is in Washington, D.C.

7. _F_ Pterodactyls are alive now.

8. _F_ Pterodactyl fossils have not been found.

9. What did the Smithsonian do with the model? __tested it to see if an animal that large could fly__ (Answers may vary.)

10. How did Pat know for sure they were flying over Washington, D.C.? __She saw familiar sights.__ (Answers may vary.)

Working with Words

The suffix **-able** or **-ible** means "capable of" or "tending to." Write the words from the story that have this suffix and that are formed from these base words.

1. horror __horrible__ (Par. 3)

2. believe __unbelievable__ (Par. 9)

3. reason __reasonable__ (Par. 17)

11

Knowing the Words

Write the words from the story that have the meanings below.

1. dealing with muscles __muscular__ (Par. 6)

2. differ from __vary__ (Par. 6)

3. cover over __overlap__ (Par. 8)

4. group acting as one __unit__ (Par. 10)

5. ability __capacity__ (Par. 11)

In each row below, circle the two words that are related to the word in dark print.

6. **bird** pterodactyl (condor) (eagle)

7. **airplane** (fuselage) (throttle) fossil

8. **people** (dispatcher) terminal (parent)

9. **skeleton** (backbone) muscles (skull)

10. **feathers** skull (wing) (tail)

Working with Words

Possessives are words that show ownership. The singular possessive is usually formed by adding 's to a noun. Rewrite each phrase below. Use possessive forms.

1. the wings of a bird __a bird's wings__

2. the body of an animal __an animal's body__

3. the hat that belongs to Charlie __Charlie's hat__

4. the message of the dispatcher __the dispatcher's message__

Write the compound words from the story that are formed by adding to these words.

5. back __backbone__ (Par. 4)

6. lap __overlap__ (Par. 8)

Reading and Thinking

1. Check the features that are common to birds as opposed to other animals.
   - ✓ They have paper-thin skulls.
   - ____ Their bones are filled with tissue.
   - ✓ They have strong, short backbones.
   - ✓ They have wing and tail feathers.

2. Check the sentence that best expresses the main idea of this story.
   - ____ Feathers help birds fly.
   - ✓ A bird is designed for flying.
   - ____ Birds are different from reptiles.

3. Check the most likely conclusion you can make about Pat.
   - ✓ She was interested in flight in the sixth grade.
   - ____ She knew a lot about reptiles.
   - ____ She likes to save school papers.

Learning to Study

This graph shows the lengths of some birds. Under each bar on the graph, write the letter of the bird whose size is represented.

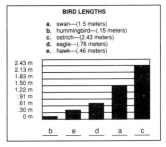

BIRD LENGTHS	
a.	swan—(1.5 meters)
b.	hummingbird—(.15 meters)
c.	ostrich—(2.43 meters)
d.	eagle—(.76 meters)
e.	hawk—(.46 meters)

2.43 m, 2.13 m, 1.83 m, 1.50 m, 1.22 m, .91 m, .61 m, .30 m, 0 m

b   e   d   a   c

13

Knowing the Words

Write the words from the story that have the meanings below.

1. surfaces designed to lift a plane __airfoils__ (Par. 4)

2. devices with revolving blades used to move a boat or plane __propellers__ (Par. 4)

3. go against __counteract__ (Par. 5)

4. air pressure making a plane rise __lift__ (Par. 6)

5. allow __enable__ (Par. 8)

6. Check the sentence in which *drag* has the same meaning as in paragraph 5.
   - ____ The minutes will drag until dinner.
   - ✓ The drag on the car forced the engine to work harder.
   - ____ Can the horses drag the tractor out of the snowdrift?

7. Check the sentence in which *thrust* has the same meaning as in paragraph 5.
   - ____ Spot thrust his way out the door.
   - ____ I thrust the pin into the balloon.
   - ✓ The propeller created enough thrust to get the boat off the sandbar.

Working with Words

The suffix **-ward** means "in the direction of." Write the words from the story that have the suffix **-ward** and that are formed from these base words.

1. fore __forward__ (Par. 5)

2. down __downward__ (Par. 6)

3. to __toward__ (Par. 6)

4. up __upward__ (Par. 7)

Reading and Thinking

Write the word that best completes each sentence.

1. Gravity and drag are natural, __physical__ forces.
   adjoining   hazardous   physical

2. Air __pressure__ creates lift.
   capacity   pressure   maneuver

3. The pilot increased engine power to create more __thrust__.
   drag   gravity   thrust

Write **B** before statements that describe birds, write **P** before those that describe planes, and write **B/P** before statements that describe both.

4. _B/P_ They have curved wings.

5. _B_ They have feathers.

6. _P_ They have propellers.

7. _P_ They have engines.

8. _B/P_ They use lift and thrust to oppose gravity and drag.

Learning to Study

Different references provide different types of information. Write the name of the best reference to find each piece of information.

atlas   almanac   newspaper
dictionary   encyclopedia

1. how an airplane flies __encyclopedia__

2. definition of *airfoil* __dictionary__

3. map of Washington, D.C. __atlas__

4. facts about airport sizes __almanac__

5. weather forecast __newspaper__

15

Knowing the Words

Write the words from the story that have the meanings below.

1. side to side movement of the nose of a plane __yaw__ (Par. 4)

2. vertical flat piece on a plane's tail assembly causing yaw __rudder__ (Par. 4)

3. hinged parts on plane wings that make the plane roll __ailerons__ (Par. 5)

4. lever that operates the elevators and ailerons __yoke__ (Par. 5)

5. part of a plane's tail assembly that causes pitch __elevator__ (Par. 6)

6. up and down movement of the nose of a plane __pitch__ (Par. 6)

Synonyms are words that have the same or nearly the same meanings. Write the words from the story that are synonyms for these words.

7. rolling __banking__ (Par. 5)

8. pilot's stick __yoke__ (Par. 5)

9. laws __regulations__ (Par. 12)

Working with Words

The possessive of a plural word that ends in s is formed by adding an apostrophe after the s. For example, the plural possessive form of *friend* is *friends'*. Write a sentence that includes the plural possessive form of each word below. (Sentences will vary.)

1. plane __planes'__

2. pilot __pilots'__

3. rudder __rudders'__

Reading and Thinking

1. What might happen if a pilot used only one control to make a maneuver? __The plane could skid.__

2. Check the sentence that best expresses the main idea of this story.
   - ✓ A pilot must know a lot.
   - ____ A plane has four basic controls.
   - ____ A plane has three basic movements.

3. A **summary** briefly gives facts about a topic. To summarize, you must find the most important facts and put them in an order that makes sense. In one sentence, summarize the information in paragraph 5. __A pilot can make a plane roll or bank.__ (Answers may vary.)

Learning to Study

An **outline** is a form that shows how the important points in an article are related. Complete this partial outline for paragraphs 4 through 6 of this story.

I. Airplane Movements
   A. Yaw
      1. Plane Control: __rudder__
      2. Pilot's Control: __rudder pedal__
   B. Roll or Bank
      1. Plane Control: __ailerons__
      2. Pilot's Control: __yoke__
   C. Pitch
      1. Plane Control: __elevator__
      2. Pilot's Control: __yoke__

17

Write the words from the story that have the meanings below.

1. story or legend _____ myth _____ (Par. 5)

2. confusing network of paths _____ maze _____ (Par. 7)

3. put in jail _____ imprisoned _____ (Par. 8)

4. substance that holds things together _____ adhesive _____ (Par. 10)

Write the actual meanings of these idioms.

5. *out of the blue* _____ unexpectedly _____

6. *I'm all ears* _____ tell me _____
(Answers may vary.)

7. Check the sentence in which *figure* has the same meaning as in paragraph 3.
_____ Divide this figure into that one to get the answer.
✓ Did you figure out the mystery?
_____ There was one lonely figure in the painting.

8. Check the sentence in which *right* has the same meaning as in paragraph 11.
_____ Turn right at the corner.
_____ The magazine was right there on the table.
✓ You were right about the situation.

The prefix **im-** often means "not." Write the meaning of each word below.

1. impatient _____ not patient _____

2. immature _____ not mature _____

3. impossible _____ not possible _____

4. impolite _____ not polite _____

1. Check the word that best describes the feeling or mood of the atmosphere in the cockpit.
_____ scary _____ humorous
✓ relaxed _____ tense

2. Check the word that best describes Minos.
_____ ugly ✓ cruel
_____ funny _____ skillful

3. What do you think made Charlie think of the story about Daedalus and Icarus?
He was thinking about flying close to
the sun. (Answers may vary.)

4. Check the conclusion you can make about the flying weather in this story.
_____ The sky was dark and stormy.
_____ The sky was full of snow.
✓ There was a clear blue sky.

5. How hot is the sun?
ten thousand degrees Fahrenheit

1. To find out more about Icarus, Daedalus, and King Minos, you could use reference sources. Put a **1** before the best source of this information. Put a **2** before the second-best source.
_____ almanac 2 encyclopedia
_____ newspaper _____ dictionary
_____ atlas 1 a book of myths

Write the names of two reference sources you could use to find facts about the sun.

2. _____ almanac _____

3. _____ encyclopedia _____

Write the words from the story that have the meanings below.

1. in the air _____ afloat _____ (Par. 4)

2. science of flight _____ aeronautics _____ (Par. 5)

3. aircraft with two sets of wings _____ biplane _____ (Par. 5)

4. recognize _____ acknowledge _____ (Par. 8)

5. special and unusual _____ unique _____ (Par. 9)

6. airplane flight _____ aviation _____ (Par. 9)

An **antonym** is a word that is opposite in meaning from another word. Write the words from the story that are antonyms for these words.

7. sunk _____ floated _____ (Par. 4)

8. fixed _____ damaged _____ (Par. 7)

9. gave _____ received _____ (Par. 8)

10. failures _____ achievements _____ (Par. 8)

The suffix **-ful** means "full of." Write the words from the story with the suffix **-ful** that are formed from these base words.

1. success _____ successfully _____ (Par. 3)

2. power _____ powerful _____ (Par. 8)

Write the words that have the suffix **-ful** and the meanings below.

3. full of grace _____ graceful _____

4. full of use _____ useful _____

5. full of help _____ helpful _____

6. full of cheer _____ cheerful _____

7. full of fear _____ fearful _____

1. Check the conclusions you could make based on the fact that the Wright brothers took their airplane invention Europe.
✓ They thought they had an important invention.
_____ They could speak French.
✓ They were frustrated with the lack of recognition in the United State

2. Why did the Wright brothers design a biplane rather than a plane with only one set of wings?
They had tested a two-winged glider.
(Answers may vary.)

3. Number the events to show the order which they happened.
6 The United States acknowledged the Wright brothers' achievement
4 A gust of wind damaged the *Flyer*
1 The brothers opened a bicycle shop.
3 The brothers built the *Flyer* and tested it at Kitty Hawk.
5 The brothers went to Europe.
2 The brothers built a glider.

Refer to the pronunciation key on the inside back cover of this book to write the words that each of these respellings represents.

1. /ak nol′ ij/ _____ acknowledge _____

2. /ar′ ə nòt iks/ _____ aeronautics _____

3. /ā′ lə ron′/ _____ aileron _____

4. /yü nēk′/ _____ unique _____

5. /yó/ _____ yaw _____

Write the words from the story that have the meanings below.

1. blow up or swell with air or gas _____ inflate _____ (Par. 3)

2. quality of something _____ property _____ (Par. 3)

3. round figure _____ sphere _____ (Par. 4)

4. colorless gas that burns easily _____ hydrogen _____ (Par. 5)

5. Check the sentence in which *property* has the same meaning as in paragraph 3.
_____ That book is my own property.
_____ We own property in Utah.
✓ Lemon juice has a sour property.

6. Check the sentence in which *rose* has the same meaning as in paragraph 5.
_____ Ross gave Pat a yellow rose.
✓ The smoke rose.
_____ Your skirt is a rose color.

The prefix **in-** can mean "in, within, toward, into," or "on." Write the words from the story that have the prefix **in-** and come from these foreign base words.

1. *spirare*, meaning "to breathe" _____ inspired _____ (Par. 3)

2. *flare*, meaning "blow" _____ inflate _____ (Par. 3)

3. *sid*, meaning "wide" _____ inside _____ (Par. 4)

Rewrite each phrase below. Use possessive forms.

4. the balloon of the Montgolfier brothers
the Montgolfier brothers' balloon

5. the record for the world
the world's record

Write **T** before the statements that are true. Write **F** before those that are false.

1. T Hot-air balloons were flown before hydrogen balloons were flown.

2. F The first hot-air balloon was fifteen feet wide.

3. F The Montgolfiers used hydrogen to inflate the first balloon.

4. T Hot-air balloons are flown today.

5. F The Montgolfiers were English.

6. Why did the people of the village where the first hydrogen balloon landed tear the balloon to bits?
They had never seen anything like it
before. (Answers may vary.)

7. In one sentence, summarize the ballooning events of 1783.
The first hot-air, hydrogen, and
passenger balloons were launched in
1783. (Answers may vary.)

Guide words are the two words in dark print at the top of each page of a dictionary. These words are helpful in finding words quickly. Write the words from the list that would appear on a dictionary page that has each of these sets of guide words below.

sphere inflate hydrogen property

1. **helm—imprisoned** _____ hydrogen _____

2. **prehistoric—punctual** _____ property _____

3. **immature—inspired** _____ inflate _____

4. **spectacular—throttle** _____ sphere _____

Write the words from the story that have the meanings below.

1. colorless gas that does not burn _____ helium _____ (Par. 2)

2. crossing the Atlantic Ocean _____ transatlantic _____ (Par. 2)

3. upward movement _____ ascent _____ (Par. 6)

4. unable to feel _____ numb _____ (Par. 6)

5. part that regulates flow _____ valve _____ (Par. 6)

6. brought back to consciousness _____ revived _____ (Par. 6)

Write the words from the story that are **antonyms** (words that mean the opposite of) these words.

7. descent _____ ascent _____ (Par. 6)

8. alert _____ dazed _____ (Par. 7)

9. unconsciousness _____ awareness _____ (Par. 9)

The suffix **-ness** means "condition" or "quality." Write the words from the story that have the suffix **-ness** and the meanings below.

1. quality of being numb _____ numbness _____ (Par. 6)

2. quality of being aware _____ awareness _____ (Par. 9)

3. unconscious condition _____ unconsciousness _____ (Par. 9)

4. useful quality _____ usefulness _____ (Par. 11)

Choose two words with the suffix **-ness** from above and write a sentence for each.

5. _____ (Answers will vary.) _____

6. _____

1. Write the word that best completes this sentence.
The valve _____ released _____ hydrogen from the balloon.
released revived imprisoned

2. Check the sentence that best expresses the main idea of this story.
✓ Pat has learned a lot about balloons.
_____ Ballooning helped people learn about oxygen.
_____ Ballooning helped people learn a about the weather.

Write **F** for fact or **O** for opinion before each statement below.

3. F Dorothea Klumpke was the first woman to study the sky from a balloon.

4. O Early balloonists were brave.

5. F Hydrogen is lighter than air.

6. F Lack of oxygen causes unconsciousness.

7. Check the most likely reason the autho had for writing this article.
_____ to entertain
✓ to inform
_____ to persuade

Complete this partial outline for the helium balloon records mentioned in the story.

Balloon Flight Records

I. First Transatlantic Flight

II. First Nonstop Crossing of North America

III. First Crossing of the Pacific Ocean

IV. First Solo Transatlantic Flight

Knowing the Words

Write the words from the story that have the meanings below.

1. airship _____ dirigible _____ (Par. 3)
2. sudden _____ abrupt _____ (Par. 4)
3. rigid airships named for their inventor _____ zeppelins _____ (Par. 6)
4. places for anchoring _____ mooring masts _____ (Par. 8)
5. nonrigid airship _____ blimp _____ (Par. 10)

In each row below, circle the two words that are related to the word in dark print.

6. **airship** (blimp) fuselage (zeppelin)
7. **hydrogen** (helium) (oxygen) platform

8. Check the sentence in which *promise* has the same meaning as in paragraph 5.
_____ I promise to return your magazine.
_____ I will keep my promise.
✓ This student shows promise.

Working with Words

The prefix **dis-** means "not" or "opposite of." Write the words that have the prefix **dis-** and the meanings below.

1. not honest _____ dishonest _____
2. not appeared _____ disappeared _____
3. not an advantage _____ disadvantage _____
4. not approved _____ disapproved _____
5. not courteous _____ discourteous _____

Write the compound words from the story that are formed by adding to these words.

6. air _____ airships _____ (Par. 6)
7. back _____ backyard _____ (Par. 12)

Reading and Thinking

Write the word that best completes each sentence.

1. The *Hindenburg* should have used a _____ nonflammable _____ gas.
flammable   nonflammable   hydrogen

2. Airships needed huge _____ hangars _____.
hangars   zeppelins   dirigibles

3. The boat tried to _____ dock _____ at the harbor.
burst   advance   dock

Write two of the reasons airships have almost disappeared.

4. They are too slow and inefficient.
5. They are too fragile.
(Answers may vary.)

6. Check the most likely conclusion you can make based on the fact that a nonflammable gas was used after the *Hindenburg* was destroyed.
_____ Airship travel grew.
✓ Airship travel was safer.
_____ Airship travel took more time.
_____ Airship travel was abandoned.

Learning to Study

The *Readers' Guide to Periodical Literature* is a book that contains a listing of a large number of magazine articles. The article subjects are arranged alphabetically. A new list comes out monthly. Below are four topics. Check the ones with which the *Readers' Guide* could be most helpful.

_____ the first balloon flight
_____ the *Hindenburg*
✓ the latest balloon flight record
✓ new developments in aviation

27

Knowing the Words

Write the words from the story that have the meanings below.

1. upward air movement _____ updraft _____ (Par. 11)
2. causing a change in direction _____ deflecting _____ (Par. 11)
3. glider _____ sailplane _____ (Par. 16)
4. take apart _____ dismantle _____ (Par. 17)

A **pun** is a play on two words that sound alike or one word that has a double meaning. Pat used two puns in this story. Write the word that each pun refers to.

5. in one piece _____ peace _____ (Par. 8)
6. made me sore _____ soar _____ (Par. 20)

Write the words from the story that are synonyms (words that have the same or nearly the same meanings) for these words.

7. pull _____ tow _____ (Par. 2)
8. jerk _____ jolt _____ (Par. 16)
9. field _____ pasture _____ (Par. 18)
10. examining _____ investigating _____ (Par. 18)

Working with Words

The prefix **in-** can mean "in, within, toward, into," or "on." It can also mean "not." Write the words from the story in which **in-** means "in" or "on" and that come from these foreign base words.

1. *dicare,* meaning "dedicate" _____ indication _____ (Par. 11)
2. *vestigium,* meaning "footprint" or "track" _____ investigating _____ (Par. 18)

Write the words from the story in which **in-** means "not."

3. _____ insecure _____ (Par. 3)   4. _____ incredible _____ (Par. 14)

Reading and Thinking

Write **G** before statements that describe gliders, write **A** before statements that describe airplanes, and write **G/A** before statements that describe both.

1. G/A They have wings and a fuselage.
2. G/A They are heavier than air.
3. A They use engines to propel them.
4. G They use updrafts to gain altitude.
5. G/A They have landing gear.

6. Check the word that best describes the weather in this story.
_____ stormy   _____ foggy
✓ sunny   _____ cloudy

7. Check the most likely story outcome.
_____ Pat will never go soaring again.
_____ Pat will take Charlotte on an adventurous airplane trip.
✓ Pat will go soaring again.

8. Why do you think the sailplane was so quiet you could hear a pin drop?
It had no engine.

Learning to Study

The *Readers' Guide to Periodical Literature* is a book that contains a listing of magazine articles on many subjects. Use this sample listing to answer the questions below.

Soaring
The Wings of the Wind. J. Rubin. il.
Sport and Leisure 132:117-24, O 14 '87.

1. What is the subject? _____ soaring _____
2. What is the title of the article?
The Wings of the Wind
3. What is the date it was published?
October 14, 1987

29

Knowing the Words

Write the words from the story that have the meanings below.

1. fascinated _____ intrigued _____ (Par. 1)
2. special notice _____ recognition _____ (Par. 5)
3. bit of evidence _____ trace _____ (Par. 8)
4. far reaching _____ extensive _____ (Par. 8)
5. guess _____ speculate _____ (Par. 9)

Write the words from the story that are represented by these abbreviations.

6. U.S. _____ United States _____ (Par. 2)
7. KS _____ Kansas _____ (Par. 3)
8. CA _____ California _____ (Par. 3)
9. Atl. _____ Atlantic _____ (Par. 5)
10. Pac. _____ Pacific _____ (Par. 6)
11. FL _____ Florida _____ (Par. 7)
12. Is. _____ Island _____ (Par. 8)

Learning to Study

Below is a map showing the area where Earhart's plane vanished. Look at the map and then fill in the information.

1. Starting point _____ Lae, New Guinea _____
2. Intended destination _____ Howland Island _____
3. Direction headed _____ east or northeast _____

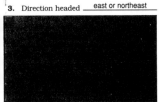

Reading and Thinking

1. Number the events to show the order in which they happened to Earhart.
3 She flew solo across the Atlantic.
4 She tried to fly around the world.
1 She worked as a nurse.
6 George Putnam wrote her story.
2 She became the first woman to cross the Atlantic.
5 She vanished with no trace.

2. Check the sentence that best expresses the main idea of this story.
_____ Fame came to Earhart in 1928.
✓ Earhart was a remarkable person.
_____ Earhart was the first woman to fly solo across the Atlantic.

Write **F** for fact or **O** for opinion before each statement below.

3. O Earhart's flying skills were excellent.
4. F Earhart married a publisher.
5. F Earhart became the first woman to fly across the Atlantic Ocean.
6. O Amelia Earhart was the greatest pilot.

Working with Words

Write the compound words from the story that are formed by adding to these words.

1. ordinary _____ extraordinary _____ (Par. 2)
2. night _____ overnight _____ (Par. 5)

Write the words from the story that contain the suffixes below.

3. -y _____ risky _____ (Par. 2)
4. -ly _____ friendly _____ (Par. 4)

31

Knowing the Words

Write the words from the story that have the meanings below.

1. entered _____ enrolled _____ (Par. 2)
2. crossing of a continent _____ transcontinental _____ (Par. 5)
3. terrible situation _____ tragedy _____ (Par. 8)
4. public recognition _____ publicity _____ (Par. 8)
5. natural surroundings _____ environment _____ (Par. 9)

Write the phrases from the story that are idioms and have these meanings.

6. exaggerated _____ larger than life _____ (Par. 6)
7. being famous _____ in the public eye _____ (Par. 6)
8. through her own efforts _____ in her own right _____ (Par. 7)

Write the words from the story that are synonyms (words that have the same or nearly the same meanings) for these words.

9. alone _____ solo _____ (Par. 4)
10. trips _____ expeditions _____ (Par. 7)

Working with Words

The suffix **-er** can mean "identity of." Write the words from the story that have the suffix **-er** and the meanings below.

1. one who helps _____ helper _____ (Par. 3)
2. one who advises _____ adviser _____ (Par. 9)

The suffix **-er** can also mean "more." Write the words from the story that have **-er** and the meanings below.

3. more large _____ larger _____ (Par. 6)
4. more old _____ older _____ (Par. 9)

Reading and Thinking

Write **T** before sentences that are true. Write **F** before those that are false.

1. T Charles Lindbergh made the first nonstop, solo, transatlantic flight.
2. F Charles Lindbergh knew the Wright brothers.
3. F Charles Lindbergh had not flown before winning the $25,000 prize.
4. T Anne Lindbergh was an author.
5. Check the words that describe Charles Lindbergh.
✓ daring   _____ mysterious
_____ cruel   ✓ skillful
_____ shy   _____ fearful

6. Why hadn't a nonstop, transatlantic flight been made before 1927?
Pilots became too tired and had to stop for fuel. (Answers may vary.)

Learning to Study

A time line shows the order of events. Use this time line of part of Charles Lindbergh's life to answer the questions below.

		Army Air Service			
				Transatlantic Flight	
Birth		Flight School		Marriage	
1900 1905	1910 1915	1920 1925	1930	1935 1940	

1. What amount of time is represented in this time line? _____ 40 years _____
2. Read the events below. Then check those furthest apart in the time line.
_____ Flight School and Marriage
✓ Birth and Flight School
_____ Army Air Service and Marriage

33

Knowing the Words

Write the words from the story that have the meanings below.

1. outstanding ___notable___
   (Par. 2)

2. something that blocks the way ___barrier___
   (Par. 6)

3. relating to sound ___sonic___
   (Par. 6)

4. daring accomplishment ___feat___
   (Par. 12)

Hyperbole is a figure of speech in which exaggeration is used to make a point. For example, if something were heavy, someone might say, "It weighs a ton!" On the first line below, write the phrase in the story that is an example of hyperbole. Underneath, write the true meaning of each phrase.

5. ___for a million dollars___
   (Par. 2)
   ___They don't want to do it again.___

6. ___smaller than a bathtub___
   (Par. 5)
   ___The cabin was very small.___
   (Answers may vary.)

Working with Words

Rewrite each phrase below. Use possessive forms.

1. the notable flights of Amelia Earhart
   ___Amelia Earhart's notable flights___

2. the voyage of the *Daedalus*
   ___the *Daedalus's* voyage___

3. the Mohave Desert of California
   ___California's Mohave Desert___

4. the records of aviators
   ___aviators' records___

5. the flight of Chuck Yeager
   ___Chuck Yeager's flight___

Reading and Thinking

1. What can you conclude based on the fact that Rutan and Yeager flew a longer distance around the world than Brooke Knapp did?
   ___Rutan and Yeager took a longer route.___
   ___(Answers may vary.)___

2. Check the phrase that best expresses the main idea of Pat's article.
   ✓ Flight Records
   ___ Famous Aviators
   ___ The Dream of Flight

3. Check the most likely prediction you can make based on the information in this story.
   ✓ More records will be broken.
   ___ No more records will be made.
   ___ Existing records won't be broken.

4. In one sentence, summarize paragraph 5.
   ___Rutan and Yeager flew around___
   ___the world without refueling in 1986.___
   ___(Answers may vary.)___

Learning to Study

Complete this partial outline for the article you just read. The first one is done for you.

I. Round-the-World Flight Records
   A. 1924 First Flight
   B. 1964 First Woman Solo
   C. 1984 Fastest Flight
   D. 1986 First Without Refueling
II. Sonic Barrier Records
   A. 1947 First Man
   B. 1953 First Woman

Knowing the Words

Write the words from the story that have the meanings below.

1. separate or special ___particular___
   (Par. 1)

2. engine-powered hang glider ___ultralight___
   (Par. 1)

3. measure of engine power ___horsepower___
   (Par. 4)

4. conditions ___circumstances___
   (Par. 8)

5. teasing ___taunting___
   (Par. 14)

Personification is a figure of speech in which an author writes about an idea or thing as if it had lifelike or human qualities. For example, in paragraph 12, the glider was personified when it "sprang to life" because a glider cannot be alive. Write the words or phrases that show how these objects or animals are personified in this story.

6. engine ___faithful___
   (Par. 12)

7. sun ___smiling___
   (Par. 13)

8. hawk ___laughed as if to say, taunting___
   (Par. 14)

Working with Words

The prefix **ad-** means "to" or "toward." Write the words from the list that come from these foreign base words.

admit   adjoining   adhesive   advance

1. *ante*, meaning "before" ___advance___

2. *mittere*, meaning "to send" ___admit___

3. *haerere*, meaning "to stick" ___adhesive___

4. *jungere*, meaning "to join" ___adjoining___

Reading and Thinking

1. Check the statement that best describes Pat in this story.
   ___ She will not try new things.
   ___ She loves to try new things.
   ___ She will try something new once but will not try it again.
   ✓ She may be afraid, but she will try new things anyway.

2. Why can't you find the word *ultralight* in an older dictionary?
   ___Ultralights were invented only recently.___
   ___(Answers may vary.)___

Write **T** before statements that are true. Write **F** before those that are false.

3. _F_ Ultralights weigh less than hang gliders.
4. _T_ Ultralights have small engines.
5. _T_ Some ultralights can fly as high as ten thousand feet.
6. _F_ Ultralights can travel at supersonic speeds.

7. Check the facts below that contribute to the safety of ultralights.
   ✓ They don't travel very fast.
   ___ They are reasonably inexpensive.
   ✓ They land slowly and gently.
   ___ They were invented recently.
   ✓ They don't carry much fuel.

Learning to Study

An encyclopedia has a lot of information. Check the subjects you could look up in an encyclopedia to learn about ultralights.
   ✓ Aviation   ___ Aircraft
   ___ World War II   ___ Kitty Hawk

Knowing the Words

Write the words from the story that have the meanings below.

1. people who travel back and forth from work ___commuters___
   (Par. 2)

2. courage ___nerve___
   (Par. 6)

3. airport designed for helicopters ___heliport___
   (Par. 6)

4. spinning airfoil ___rotor___
   (Par. 9)

Write the words from the story that are synonyms (words that have the same or nearly the same meanings) for these words.

5. distant ___remote___
   (Par. 5)

6. remarkable ___extraordinary___
   (Par. 7)

7. useful ___practical___
   (Par. 8)

8. spins ___rotates___
   (Par. 9)

Write the two synonyms that are used in the story for the word *helicopter.*

9. ___chopper___
   (Par. 5)

10. ___eggbeater___
    (Par. 10)

Working with Words

The suffix **-less** means "without" or "not having." Write the words with the suffix **-less** that are formed from these base words.

1. help ___helpless___
2. weight ___weightless___
3. motion ___motionless___

Write the meaning of each word below.

4. effortless ___without effort___
5. doubtless ___without doubt___
6. childless ___without children___

Reading and Thinking

Write two things about helicopters that make them practical.

1. ___They don't require runways.___

2. ___They move forward, backward, or sideways.___
   ___(Answers may vary.)___

3. Why don't the two rotors of the helicopter turn in the same direction?
   ___The helicopter would whirl out of control.___
   ___(Answers may vary.)___

Write **H** before statements that describe a helicopter, and write **A** before statements that describe an airplane.

4. _A_ requires a runway
5. _A_ has wings
6. _H_ can stay in one spot in the air
7. _H_ can move straight up and down

8. Check the most likely conclusion about helicopters you can make.
   ___ They are easy to repair.
   ✓ They are unique among aircraft.
   ___ They are not practical.

Learning to Study

Dictionary entry words are often divided into syllables. This shows where the words should be divided at the end of a line of writing. Write the words below, and leave spaces between the syllables.

1. helicopter ___hel i cop ter___

2. directions ___di rec tions___

3. A **thesaurus** is a type of dictionary in which synonyms are grouped. Check the words you might look up in a thesaurus to find synonyms for *helicopter.*
   ✓ aircraft   ___ airport
   ✓ helicopter   ___ aviator

Knowing the Words

Write the words from the story that have the meanings below.

1. upkeep ___maintenance___
   (Par. 1)

2. faster than the speed of sound ___supersonic___
   (Par. 4)

3. ordinary ___commonplace___
   (Par. 4)

4. having to do with your surroundings ___environmental___
   (Par. 6)

5. answer ___solution___
   (Par. 11)

6. space vehicle ___shuttle___
   (Par. 12)

7. Check the sentence in which *iron* has the same meaning as in paragraph 6.
   ___ Take the iron out of the box.
   ✓ Tom needs to iron out the bugs in his invention.
   ___ You should iron that shirt.

In each row below, circle the two words that are related.

8. (transports)   problems   (airliners)
9. delay   (speed)   (supersonic)

Working with Words

The suffix **-al** means "relating to." Write the words from the story that have the suffix **-al** and that are formed from these base words.

1. environment ___environmental___
   (Par. 6)

2. practice ___practical___
   (Par. 10)

Write the words that have the suffix **-al** and the meanings below.

3. relating to economy ___economical___

4. relating to fiction ___fictional___

5. relating to politics ___political___

Reading and Thinking

Write the word that best completes each sentence.

1. Large numbers of people flying can cause ___overcrowded___ airports.
   complete   overcrowded   practical

2. Careful thought is needed to find ___solutions___ to problems.
   passengers   delays   solutions

3. Check the sentence that best expresses the main idea of this story.
   ✓ The aviation industry is giving clues about the future of aviation.
   ___ Some planes can travel more than two times the speed of sound.
   ___ Early aviators did not dream the planes would lead to the aircraft today.

4. Check the most likely reason the author had for writing this story.
   ___ to entertain
   ✓ to inform
   ___ to persuade

Learning to Study

The signs below are currently used to help travelers locate necessary services. Match the signs with the services below.

1. _d_ ticket purchases   a.
2. _a_ car rental   b.
3. _f_ restaurant   c.
4. _e_ information   d.
5. _c_ air transportation   e.
6. _b_ baggage   f.

Knowing the Words

Write the words from the story that have the meanings below.

1. supporting _sponsoring_ (Par. 2)
2. interested people _enthusiasts_ (Par. 6)
3. sending up or out _launching_ (Par. 9)
4. ability to last _endurance_ (Par. 11)

In each row below, circle the two words that are related.

5. (enormous) (huge) ridiculous
6. (flexible) triangular (bowed)

Find and write the idioms in the story that are figurative ways of saying these phrases.

7. "leave me alone"
go fly a kite (Par. 1)

8. "help me" _give me a hand_ (Par. 9)

9. Check the sentence in which *mean* has the same meaning as in paragraph 12.
   - [✓] Did you mean what you said?
   - [ ] That dog is not really mean.
   - [ ] That woman flies a mean kite.

Working with Words

Hyphenated compound words are formed by putting two or more words together with hyphens to make a new word. Write the hyphenated compound words from the story that are formed by adding a word or words to each word below.

1. old _old-fashioned_ (Par. 2)
2. diamond _diamond-shaped_ (Par. 7)
3. five _fifty-five_ (Par. 10)
4. year _twelve-year-old_ (Par. 11)

Reading and Thinking

1. Check the word that best describes the mood of this story.
   - [ ] scary
   - [✓] pleasant
   - [ ] humorous
   - [ ] tense

2. Check the sentence that best expresses the main idea of this story.
   - [✓] Charlie attended a kite festival.
   - [ ] Kites were invented in Asia.
   - [ ] There are many types of kites.

Write **F** for fact or **O** for opinion before each statement below.

3. _O_ Kites are colorful.
4. _F_ Kites were invented in Asia.
5. _F_ Kites have been used in scientific experiments.
6. _O_ A ten-mile-an-hour wind is perfect for kite flying.

7. Check the most likely outcome of this story.
   - [✓] Charlie will want to attend next year's kite festival.
   - [ ] Pat will make a kite of her own.
   - [ ] Pat won't want to attend any more kite festivals.

Learning to Study

Read this classified advertisement from the newspaper and answer the questions below.

For Sale: Flexible silk kite. 8'x10'. $150 firm. Call 555-4553 after 5:00 P.M.

1. What is the cost of the kite? _$150_
2. What type of kite is it? _flexible silk_
3. How large is the kite? _8'x10'_
4. When can you call? _after 5:00 P.M._

Knowing the Words

Write the words from the story that have the meanings below.

1. measures taken to prevent harm _precautions_ (Par. 3)
2. scornfully _sarcastically_ (Par. 8)
3. to have received the right to produce an invention _patented_ (Par. 9)
4. agreement _unison_ (Par. 15)

Write the words from the story that are synonyms (words that have the same or nearly the same meanings) for these words.

5. persuaded _convinced_ (Par. 1)
6. honestly _frankly_ (Par. 5)

Write the phrases from the story that suggest hyperbole or exaggeration and have these intended meanings.

7. jump off a hill
jump off a mile-high mountain cliff (Par. 5)

8. Pat doesn't want to jump very high.
Pat would reach about a two-inch altitude. (Par. 7)

Working with Words

Many words can use more than one suffix. Write the words that can be formed by adding the suffixes below to these base words. You may have to change the spelling of the base word before adding a suffix.

	-ful	-ly
1. beauty	beautiful	beautifully
2. grace	graceful	gracefully
3. fear	fearful	fearfully
4. thank	thankful	thankfully

Reading and Thinking

Write the word that best completes each sentence.

1. Hang gliders are made from aluminum and _synthetic_ materials.
   sarcastic   synthetic   innocent

2. I _assure_ you that you are perfectly right.
   convince   acknowledge   assure

3. Do you think Pat will really try hang gliding? Explain. _____
   (Answers will vary.)

Complete each sentence with the correct word from the story.

4. The cloth on a hang glider acts as a _sail_ (Par. 4)
5. Pilots can soar higher in a hang glider by riding an _updraft_ (Par. 12)

Learning to Study

A library's card catalog or computer reference system gives you three ways to look up information: by author, by title, or by subject. Read this reference and then answer the questions below.

```
CALL NO:    J890.23
AUTHOR:     Martin, Lise
MAIN TITLE: Hang Gliding—The Thrill of It!
PUBLISHER:  Window Press, 1995
```

1. What is the title of this book?
   Hang Gliding—The Thrill of It!
2. What is the subject? _hang gliding_
3. How can you find the book on the shelf?
   Look up the number J 890.23.

Knowing the Words

Write the words from the story that have the meanings below.

1. contest _competition_ (Par. 4)
2. length of time that something lasts _duration_ (Par. 4)
3. inventive _creative_ (Par. 5)
4. contestants in the last stage of competition _finalists_ (Par. 7)
5. group of things _category_ (Par. 9)

Write the words from the story that are antonyms (words that mean the opposite of) these words.

6. oversized _miniature_ (Par. 6)
7. hide _display_ (Par. 11)
8. except for _including_ (Par. 11)

In each row below, circle the two words that are related.

9. (cardboard) (newspaper) adhesives
10. category (contest) (competition)
11. (event) (fair) science

12. Write the meaning of the idiom *take the floor* from paragraph 10.
   speak _(Answers may vary.)_

Working with Words

Write the compound words from the story that are formed by adding to these words.

1. watch _stopwatch_ (Par. 4)
2. book _notebook_ (Par. 5)
3. card _cardboard_ (Par. 5)
4. news _newspaper_ (Par. 5)

Reading and Thinking

1. Number the events to show the order in which they happened.
   _5_ Pat announced the endurance winner.
   _1_ Pat tried hang gliding.
   _3_ Pat chose the finalists.
   _6_ The winning planes were put on display.
   _2_ Pat looked at the designs.
   _4_ The distance and design winners were announced.

2. Check the sentence that best expresses the main idea of this story.
   - [ ] There were many creative entries in the paper airplane contest.
   - [✓] Pat acted as judge for a local paper airplane contest.
   - [ ] There were three events in the paper airplane contest.

3. Check the most likely conclusion you can make as to why the paper airplane contest was held.
   - [ ] Teachers wanted to encourage paper airplane making.
   - [ ] Teachers didn't like students making paper airplanes in class.
   - [✓] Teachers thought a contest would be a good way to turn a game into a learning experience.

Learning to Study

Check the information that is necessary in an announcement for a paper airplane contest.

- [✓] judges' names
- [✓] contest rules
- [ ] previous winners
- [✓] place of contest
- [✓] contest sponsor
- [ ] news of other contests

Knowing the Words

Write the words from the story that have the meanings below.

1. copy _duplicate_ (Par. 10)
2. delicate _fragile_ (Par. 11)
3. lightweight wood _balsa_ (Par. 11)
4. model airplane that is guided by wires _control-line_ (Par. 14)
5. device for sending messages _transmitter_ (Par. 14)
6. calm endurance _patience_ (Par. 15)

Write the words from the story that are represented by these abbreviations.

7. apt. _apartment_ (Par. 2)
8. bldg. _building_ (Par. 2)
9. sch. _school_ (Par. 4)
10. cont. _continued_ (Par. 11)

Working with Words

The prefix **inter-** means "between" or "among." Write the words from the story that have the prefix **inter-** and come from these base words.

1. nation _international_ (Par. 10)
2. view _interview_ (Par. 17)

Match the words that have the prefix **inter-** with the meanings below.

   a. intersection   c. intermission
   b. interrupted   d. interfere

3. _c_ pause between acts
4. _a_ place where two things cross
5. _d_ meddle
6. _b_ broke into an ongoing activity

Reading and Thinking

1. Do you think Ramon's report will be a good one? Explain.
   (Answers will vary.)

2. Why did Stewart take his broken airplane model to Charlie?
   He knew Charlie built model airplanes.
   (Answers may vary.)

Write **F** for fact or **O** for opinion before each statement below.

3. _F_ Some model airplanes are gliders.
4. _O_ Radio-control models are the best.
5. _F_ There is more than one kind of contest for model airplanes.
6. _O_ Some models could win prizes.

7. Check the word that best describes Ramon.
   - [ ] impatient
   - [ ] quiet
   - [ ] funny
   - [✓] interested

Learning to Study

A chart helps to organize and compare information by using words or numbers. Study the chart that Ramon made for his report and then answer the questions below.

Model Airplanes	Engine Types
Display	None
Indoor	Rubber Band
Free-Flight	Rubber Band or Piston
Control-Line	Piston or Jet
Radio-Control	Electric

1. How many types of model airplanes did Ramon discover? _five_
2. Why is there no engine type for Display models? _They have no engines._
3. What four types of engines do model airplanes use?
   Rubber Band, Piston, Jet, or Electric

Knowing the Words

Write the words from the story that have the meanings below.

1. having to do with the air — aerial (Par. 3)
2. sport of parachute jumping — skydiving (Par. 4)
3. cord attached from airplane to parachute — static line (Par. 5)
4. dropping before the parachute opens — free-fall (Par. 8)
5. string that is pulled to open a parachute — ripcord (Par. 10)

Write the meanings of the idioms in this story.

6. *butterflies in their stomachs* — to be nervous
7. *beg off* — to refuse
8. *knock some sense into* — make someone be realistic
9. Find the simile in paragraph 8 and write it below. — felt like a bird flying

Working with Words

Rewrite each of the phrases below. Use possessive forms.

1. the first jump of Charlotte — Charlotte's first jump
2. the licenses of the experts — the experts' licenses
3. the biggest challenge of aviation — aviation's biggest challenge

Reading and Thinking

1. Check the most likely reason the author had for writing this story.
   - ___ to train people to skydive
   - ✓ to introduce the reader to a sport
   - ___ to make people go to air shows

2. Check the word that best describes the mood of this story.
   - ___ astonishment ___ seriousness
   - ✓ excitement ___ fearfulness

Write the word that best completes each sentence.

3. There was __absolutely__ nothing else to do but jump.
   automatically   absolutely   gently

4. When the __chute__ opened, she was relieved.
   chute   ripcord   static line

Learning to Study

Many words have more than one meaning. Dictionaries number the definitions after each entry. Use a dictionary to find two meanings for each word below.
(Answers may vary.)

1. class
   school group   category
2. elevator
   airplane part   mechanical stairs
3. Complete this partial outline of paragraph 8.
   I. Parachute jump
   A. Free-fall
   B. Chute opening
   C. Landing

Knowing the Words

Write the words from the story that have the meanings below.

1. series of actions — process (Par. 4)
2. disturbance — commotion (Par. 5)
3. director — controller (Par. 6)
4. not wasting time or effort — efficient (Par. 9)
5. Check the sentence in which *outline* has the same meaning as in paragraph 7.
   - ___ Do you see the cat's outline?
   - ✓ Trees outline the landscape.
   - ___ Write an outline before you begin writing your article.

Some words can be written in more than one way, depending on their meaning. For example, *take off* is a verb showing action, but *takeoff* is a noun. Complete each sentence with *take off* or *takeoff*.

6. The plane will __take off__ on time.
7. The pilot's __takeoff__ was perfect.

Working with Words

The prefix **com-** means "with" or "together." Write the words from the story that have the prefix **com-** and come from these foreign base words.

1. from Latin *bini*, meaning "two by two" — combined (Par. 1)
2. from Latin *munus*, meaning "service" — community (Par. 1)
3. from Latin *movēre*, meaning "to move" — commotion (Par. 5)

Reading and Thinkin

1. Check the sentence that best expres the main idea of this story.
   - ___ Passengers fly around the world
   - ✓ Many people run an airport.
   - ___ The turnaround crew gets each plane ready for takeoff.

2. In what ways can a plane be refuele
   large tank trucks or pumped
   from underground tanks
   (Answers may vary.)

3. Summarize the information in paragraph 3 in one sentence.
   The turnaround crew cleans the plane
   the ramp crew loads baggage and frei
   (Answers may vary.)

Learning to Study

Below is a help-wanted ad from the classified section of a newspaper. Read t ad and then answer the questions below

> **Airplane Mechanic:** 2 yrs. exper. with planes necessary. Must be willing to relocate. 555-4469.

1. Should people who have no mechan experience apply for this job? Why?
   No, they need two years of experience

2. Should people who want to move ap for this job? Why?
   Yes, they must be willing to relocate.

A dictionary entry word's part of speech often indicated by an abbreviation that follows the respelling. Use a dictionary t match these words to their parts of spee

3. __c__ mechanic a. preposition
4. __d__ carefully b. adjective
5. __a__ of c. noun
6. __b__ important d. adverb
7. __e__ communicate e. verb

51

Knowing the Words

Write the words from the story that have the meanings below.

1. waits on others — attendant (Par. 1)
2. ways of doing things — procedures (Par. 2)
3. smooth and rapid — fluent (Par. 4)
4. between countries — international (Par. 4)
5. stormy or disorderly — turbulent (Par. 8)

Write the words from the story that are synonyms (words that have the same or nearly the same meanings) for these words.

6. odd — unusual (Par. 1)
7. luggage — baggage (Par. 2)
8. untrained — inexperienced (Par. 3)
9. noisy — rowdy (Par. 8)

10. Check the sentence in which *checks* has the same meaning as in paragraph 2.
   - ___ I marked the papers with checks.
   - ___ We have a system of checks and balances.
   - ✓ She checks the baby hourly.

Working with Words

Both a prefix and a suffix can be added to many words. Write the words that can be created by adding the given prefix and suffix to each of the following base words.

Base	Prefix	Suffix	
1. nation	inter-	-al	international
2. usual	un-	-ly	unusually
3. event	un-	-ful	uneventful
4. friend	un-	-ly	unfriendly

Reading and Thinking

1. Number the following events to show the order in which they happen on a flight.
   - 2 Passengers are directed to seats.
   - 5 The plane takes off.
   - 1 The attendant checks the supplies.
   - 6 Meals are served.
   - 3 Safety procedures are reviewed.
   - 4 The cabin is checked for loose baggage.

2. Check the most likely reason the author had for writing this story.
   - ___ to describe a man named Arnie
   - ___ to describe a plane ride
   - ✓ to describe an attendant's job

3. What second language do you think Arnie speaks fluently? — French

4. Check the words that describe a good flight attendant.
   - ___ shy ___ rowdy
   - ✓ friendly ✓ helpful
   - ✓ efficient ✓ calm

Learning to Study

1. Complete this outline of the headings for paragraphs 2–4 of this story.
   I. Preflight duties
   II. In-flight duties
   III. Training

2. Check the references you might use to find out more about a career as a flight attendant.
   - ___ atlas ✓ card catalog
   - ___ thesaurus ✓ Readers' Guide
   - ___ almanac ✓ encyclopedia

Knowing the Words

Write the words from the story that have the meanings below.

1. people who plan and build things — engineers (Par. 1)
2. detailed descriptions — specifications (Par. 3)
3. information or facts — data (Par. 3)
4. respond — react (Par. 3)
5. shaking motion — vibration (Par. 6)
6. dealing with science that makes computers, radios, and radar work — electronic (Par. 6)

Write the words from the story that are antonyms (words that mean the opposite) of these words.

7. destructed — constructed (Par. 6)
8. under — overhead (Par. 8)

In each row below, circle the two words that are related.

9. (built) (constructed) reacted
10. (model) equipment (blueprint)
11. What does the idiom *passed with flying colors* mean in paragraph 8?
   passed successfully

Working with Words

The prefix **ir-** means "not." Write the meaning of each word below.

1. irregular — not regular
2. irresponsible — not responsible
3. irresistible — not resistible
4. irreplaceable — not replaceable
5. irreversible — not reversible

Reading and Thinkin

1. Why do you think the pilots wanted t know how the planes were tested?
   They wanted to be sure they were safe.
   (Answers may vary.)

2. In one sentence, summarize the information in paragraph 3.
   Engineers programmed a computer to
   make a mathematical model of the plane
   (Answers may vary.)

3. Check the types of airplane tests that are in the story.
   - ✓ computer test ___ history test
   - ✓ wind test ✓ flight test
   - ✓ electronic test ___ science test

Write the word that best completes each sentence.

4. The airplane's __specifications__ will be programmed into a computer.
   specifications   models   blueprin

5. The computer created the first __mathematical__ model of the pla
   atmospheric   mathematical   econom

Learning to Study

Match each reference source below with t kind of information it might contain.

a. atlas b. dictionary c. Readers' Gu
d. encyclopedia e. newspaper f. alma

1. __b__ a short definition of *blueprint*
2. __c__ the name of a magazine article recent aircraft design
3. __e__ today's temperature in Denver
4. __d__ a complete history of aeronautic engineering
5. __a__ a map of Houston, Texas
6. __f__ aircraft speed records

55

Knowing the Words

Write the words from the story that have the meanings below.

1. career _____occupation_____
(Par. 6)

2. available supplies _____resources_____
(Par. 9)

3. those who study ancient things _____archaeologists_____
(Par. 11)

4. possible _____potential_____
(Par. 11)

5. invisible rays _____infrared_____
(Par. 12)

Write the words from the story that are represented by these abbreviations.

6. AZ _____Arizona_____
(Par. 1)

7. sch. _____school_____
(Par. 1)

8. co. _____company_____
(Par. 5)

9. NY _____New York_____
(Par. 6)

10. photog. _____photographer/photography_____
(Par. 6)

11. temp. _____temperatures_____
(Par. 12)

12. HI _____Hawaii_____
(Par. 13)

13. Check the sentence in which *spot* has the same meaning as in paragraph 9.

_____ I have a spot on my sleeve.

__✓__ I can spot a mistake.

_____ From this spot, I can see it.

Working with Words

Write the closed and hyphenated compound words from the story that are formed by adding words to these words.

1. body _____somebody_____
(Par. 1)

2. known _____well-known_____
(Par. 6)

3. map _____mapmaking_____
(Par. 7)

4. camp _____campgrounds_____
(Par. 9)

Reading and Thinking

1. Check the sentence that best expresses the main idea of this story.

_____ Aerial photographers make maps.

__✓__ Aerial photography has a lot of uses.

_____ Archaeologists use aerial photos.

2. Why is it helpful for people to know if heat is escaping from buildings?

_____to know where to add insulation_____
(Answers may vary.)

3. What might be some future uses of aerial photographs?

_____
(Answers will vary.)

Learning to Study

Sometimes the spelling of a base word changes when an ending is added. In this case, a dictionary will give the irregular spelling in its entry. Use a dictionary to find the irregular spelling of the words below that have -ed and -ing added.

	-ed	-ing
1. realize	realized	realizing
2. improve	improved	improving
3. overlap	overlapped	overlapping
4. plan	planned	planning

5. Complete this outline of paragraph 11.

I. Uses of Aerial Photography

A. _____Researchers—track animals_____

B. _____Archaeologists—look for new sites_____

C. _____Cities—study pollution_____

D. _____Cities—study traffic problems_____

59

Knowing the Words

Write the words from the story that have the meanings below.

1. pass along _____relay_____
(Par. 1)

2. something not real _____illusion_____
(Par. 2)

3. not reasonable _____illogical_____
(Par. 2)

4. ditch _____trench_____
(Par. 6)

Write the metaphors from the story.

5. _____the fire would become a raging giant_____
(Par. 2)

6. _____(the fire was a) wild lion_____
(Par. 7)

7. Check the sentence in which *contain* has the same meaning as in paragraph 2.

__✓__ She could not contain her laughter when she heard the joke.

_____ Encyclopedias contain facts.

_____ This jar can contain liquid.

Working with Words

The prefix il- means "not." Form the antonym, or opposite, of the words below by adding the prefix il- to each one.

1. logical _____illogical_____

2. legal _____illegal_____

3. legible _____illegible_____

Compound words can be open, closed, or hyphenated. Write the compound words from the story that are formed by adding words to these words.

4. towers _____fire towers_____
(Par. 1)

5. out _____lookout_____
(Par. 2)

6. two _____two-way_____
(Par. 4)

7. quarters _____headquarters_____
(Par. 8)

Reading and Thinking

1. Number the events to show the order in which they happened.

__3__ Bulldozers cleared a path.

__2__ A fire alarm sounded.

__1__ A fire was out of control.

__5__ Helicopters dropped buckets of water.

__4__ Smoke jumpers reached the fire.

__6__ Everyone at headquarters felt relieved.

Write B before the statements that describe events that happened before the smoke jumpers arrived. Write A before statements that describe events that occurred after they arrived.

2. __B__ A lookout spotted a fire.

3. __A__ Planes dropped water on the fire.

4. __A__ A fire line was dug.

5. __B__ The commander looked over the situation.

6. Check the sentence that best expresses the main idea of this story.

__✓__ Fires can be fought on land and from the air.

_____ Firefighters have a risky job.

_____ Fire destroys hundreds of acres of trees each year.

Learning to Study

Refer to the pronunciation key on the inside back cover of this book. Write the word that each of these respellings represents.

1. /si chə wā´ shən/ _____situation_____

2. /zē´ rōd/ _____zeroed_____

3. /rē´ lā/ _____relay_____

4. /i kwip´ mənt/ _____equipment_____

61

Knowing the Words

Write the words from the story that have the meanings below.

necessary _____essential_____
(Par. 1)

landscape _____terrain_____
(Par. 2)

tempted _____lured_____
(Par. 4)

very cold _____frigid_____
(Par. 5)

Write the words from the story that are antonyms (words that have the same or nearly the same meanings) for these words.

wilderness _____bush_____
(Par. 1)

unafraid _____fearless_____
(Par. 9)

Learning to Study

Use this chart to answer these questions.

Wind Speed (mph)	Air Temperature (F°)			
	35°	25°	15°	5°
	Wind Chill Temperature			
4	35°	25°	15°	5°
5	32°	22°	11°	0°
10	22°	10°	–3°	–15°
15	16°	2°	–11°	–25°
20	12°	–3°	–17°	–31°

What is the wind chill temperature when wind speed is 15 mph and air temperature is 15°? _____–11°_____

What is the temperature if wind chill is -31° and wind speed is 20 mph? _____5°_____

What is the wind speed if the wind chill is 11° and the temperature is 15°? _____5 mph_____

Check the best sources for finding out about bush pilots.

_____ telephone books __✓__ card catalog

__✓__ Readers' Guide _____ atlas

__✓__ encyclopedia _____ dictionary

Reading and Thinking

Write two of the reasons that tell why it is hard to travel in Alaska.

1. _____There is a lot of wilderness._____

2. _____It's hard to build roads or railroads._____
(Answers may vary.)

3. Why is being a bush pilot dangerous?

_____They fly small planes in wilderness areas._____
(Answers may vary.)

4. Will air travel always be vital to Alaska?

Explain. _____(Answers will vary.)_____

Write F for fact or O for opinion before each statement below.

5. __O__ Bush pilots have risky jobs.

6. __F__ Alaska became a state in 1959.

7. __F__ Alaska is the largest state.

8. __O__ Flying is difficult in Alaska.

Write the word that best completes each sentence.

9. Under these _____circumstances_____ we had no choice but to jump from the plane.

departures   circumstances   frontiers

10. A big _____consideration_____ in choosing clothes is the wind chill temperature.

beginning   wilderness   consideration

Working with Words

The suffix -ure means "act or process of." Write the words that have the suffix -ure and these meanings below. You may have to drop the final e in the base word before adding the suffix.

1. act of pressing _____pressure_____

2. act of departing _____departure_____

3. act of exposing _____exposure_____

63

Knowing the Words

Write the words from the story that have the meanings below.

1. no longer useful _____obsolete_____
(Par. 2)

2. instrument with a spinning wheel inside a frame _____gyroscope_____
(Par. 5)

3. exact _____precise_____
(Par. 7)

4. responds _____reacts_____
(Par. 10)

Write the words from the story that are synonyms (words that have the same or nearly the same meanings) for these words.

5. instrument _____device_____
(Par. 5)

6. failure _____breakdown_____
(Par. 8)

Learning to Study

1. Complete this outline of paragraph 7.

I. What an autopilot contols

A. One gyroscope

1. _____ailerons_____

2. _____elevators_____

B. Second gyroscope

1. _____rudder_____

Read this airline ticket and then answer the questions below.

Passenger Name **Price, Elizabeth**			Date of Issue 12 Jan 97	
	Flight	Class	Date	Time
FROM: Nashville	4403	C	1Mar	540P
TO: Little Rock	4403	C	1Mar	840P

2. When was the ticket issued? _Jan. 12, 1997_

3. Where is Elizabeth going? _Little Rock_

4. How long is the flight? _3 hours_

5. On what date is she traveling? _March 1_

Reading and Thinking

1. Why won't pilots become obsolete?
_____(Answers will vary.)_____

2. What problem can occur if a pilot naps while the autopilot is in control?

_____The plane could miss its destination._____
(Answers may vary.)

3. Check the sentence that best expresses the main idea of this story.

_____ Autopilots are better than human pilots.

__✓__ An autopilot is a device that can steer a plane.

_____ Autopilots are like toy gyroscopes.

4. Check the most likely reason the author had for writing this story.

__✓__ to explain what an autopilot is

_____ to explain autopilot problems

_____ to explain why autopilots are better than human pilots

Write the word that best completes each sentence.

5. The toy _____gyroscope_____ spun for over a minute.

course   gyroscope   advance

6. The pilot set a _____course_____ for New Orleans.

gyroscope   cockpit   course

Working with Words

Use the possessive form of the word in parentheses in each sentence.

1. The _____group's_____ lives are in the hands of the pilot. (group)

2. Many of the _____cities'_____ problems will be solved by the subway. (cities)

65

Knowing the Words

Write the words from the story that have the meanings below.

1. special operations ___missions___
   (Par. 1)
2. useful ___practical___
   (Par. 2)
3. airplane refueling hose ___boom___
   (Par. 4)
4. meeting ___rendezvous___
   (Par. 5)
5. choice ___alternative___
   (Par. 9)

Learning to Study

Look at this map that shows some of the latitudes and longitudes of the Pacific Ocean. Then answer the questions below.

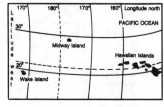

1. If planes rendezvous at 30° north latitude and 180° west longitude, what is the closest island? ___Midway Island___

2. What is the latitude and longitude of Wake Island? ___18° north latitude, 168°___
   ___west longitude___ (Answers may vary.)

3. What islands are 22° north latitude and 157° west longitude? ___Hawaiian Islands___

Write the words that these respellings represent.

4. /ron′ di vū/ ___rendezvous___

5. /mil′ ə ter′ ē/ ___military___

Reading and Thinking

1. Check the most likely conclusions you can make about how long a boom must be.
   ___ It must be three hundred feet long.
   ✓ It must be over seventy-five feet long.
   ___ It must be under eighty feet long.

2. Why don't commercial airplanes need to refuel in midair?
   ___They have enough airports.___
   (Answers may vary.)

Write **T** before sentences that are true. Write **F** before those that are false.

3. _T_ Four crew members can fly a tanker.
4. _F_ All planes must stop to refuel.
5. _T_ Tankers can assist crippled planes.
6. _F_ All in-air refueling is at night.

7. Check the sentence that best expresses the main idea of this story.
   ___ Crippled planes can be helped back to an air base.
   ___ Tankers have four crew members.
   ✓ Planes can be refueled in flight.

8. What is the difference between the job of the pilot and the job of the navigator?
   ___The pilot controls the plane, and the___
   ___navigator guides the course of the plane.___
   (Answers may vary.)

Working with Words

The suffix **-er** or **-or** can mean "identity or occupation of." Write the words with -er or -or that have these meanings.

1. one who navigates ___navigator___
2. one who operates ___operator___
3. one who controls ___controller___

Knowing the Words

Write the words from the story that have the meanings below.

1. person trained to give first aid ___paramedic___
   (Par. 1)
2. remedy ___antidote___
   (Par. 3)
3. gave or supplied ___administered___
   (Par. 7)
4. stayed in one place in the air ___hovered___
   (Par. 8)

In each row below, circle the two words that are related.

5. paramedics ⟨hikers⟩ ⟨climbers⟩
6. ⟨division⟩ unit air-rescue
7. ⟨wide-open⟩ ⟨vacant⟩ populated
8. responded ⟨spotted⟩ ⟨located⟩

Learning to Study

A **bibliography** is a list of articles or books that an author referred to when writing. Read these bibliographic entries. Then answer the questions below.

A. **Griffin, Victor.** "Mid-Air Rescue." *Aviation* Vol. 59 (October 1995): 73.

B. **Henderson, Sandra.** *Air Rescue Systems.* New York: Phantom Books, 1992.

1. Check the information given in entry **A** for a magazine article.
   ✓ page number ✓ author
   ✓ date of magazine ___ publisher
   ✓ name of magazine ✓ article title

2. Check the information given in entry **B** for a book.
   ✓ author ___ page number
   ✓ publisher ✓ publishing date
   ✓ book title ✓ city of publication

Reading and Thinking

1. Number the events to show the order which they happened.
   _2_ People searched for a missing pla
   _1_ Sam became a paramedic.
   _5_ The team went to a car accident.
   _4_ The team found a lost child.
   _6_ The team went to a hotel fire.
   _3_ Sam helped an injured pilot.

2. Check the words that describe a good rescue worker.
   ✓ concerned ___ funny
   ✓ quick-thinking ✓ reasonable

Write **F** for fact or **O** for opinion by each statement below.

3. _F_ Helicopters are used in air-rescu missions.
4. _O_ Air rescue is risky work.
5. _F_ Paramedics can give first aid.
6. _O_ It takes skill to pilot an air-rescu helicopter.

7. Why are helicopters better for air-res work than planes are?
   ___Helicopters need less space for taking___
   ___off and landing than planes do.___
   (Answers may vary.)

Working with Words

The prefix **anti-** means "against." Write th meanings of the words below that have th prefix **anti-**.

1. antigravity ___against gravity___
2. antifreeze ___against freezing___

Write the word from the story with the pre **anti-** that comes from this foreign base w

3. *didonai*, "to give" ___antidote___
   (Par. 3)

Knowing the Words

Write the words from the story that have the meanings below.

1. finding ___detecting___
   (Par. 4)
2. covering a distance ___ranging___
   (Par. 4)
3. strength ___intensity___
   (Par. 5)
4. ability to see ___visibility___
   (Par. 6)
5. small dots on radar screen that show where objects are ___blips___
   (Par. 8)
6. area ___vicinity___
   (Par. 9)
7. people who study animals ___zoologists___
   (Par. 10)
8. locate precisely ___pinpoint___
   (Par. 11)

9. Check the sentence in which *waves* has the same meaning as in paragraph 5.
   ___ The waves thundered on the beach.
   ✓ Sound travels in waves.
   ___ The operator waves the all clear.

Learning to Study

Complete this outline of the uses of radar mentioned in paragraphs 6–11.
(Answers may vary.)

I. Airplane uses
   A. Weather forecasting
   B. Avoiding accidents
   C. Plane landings
II. Scientific Uses
   A. Studying other planets
   B. Studying flight patterns of birds
III. Ship Uses
   A. Pinpointing danger

Reading and Thinking

1. What words does the acronym *radar* represent?
   ___radio detecting and ranging___

2. What two sections does a radar set have?
   ___transmitter___ ___receiver___

3. Light travels faster than sound. Check the statement below that proves this.
   ✓ After lightning is seen, thunder is heard.
   ___ Sounds are louder on a foggy day.

4. Write the main idea of this story.
   ___There are many uses for radar.___

Write the word that best completes each sentence.

5. Our ___visibility___ was blocked by the thick fog.
   intensity visibility acronym

6. The pilot tried to ___pinpoint___ the location of the collision.
   enforce assist pinpoint

Working with Words

Rewrite each phrase below. Use possessive forms.

1. the eyes of the pilots
   ___the pilots' eyes___

2. the radar screen of the tower
   ___the tower's radar screen___

3. a tool of forecasters
   ___a forecasters' tool___

4. the instructions of the control tower
   ___the control tower's instructions___

Knowing the Words

Write the words from the story that have the meanings below.

1. up and down ___vertical___
   (Par. 3)
2. inform ___snitch___
   (Par. 5)
3. cross each other ___intersect___
   (Par. 5)
4. parallel to the ground ___horizontal___
   (Par. 5)

In each row below, circle the two words that are related.

5. ⟨frantic⟩ ⟨chaos⟩ relief
6. approved ⟨alerted⟩ ⟨alarmed⟩
7. ⟨horizontal⟩ automatic ⟨vertical⟩

8. Check the sentence in which *program* has the same meaning as in paragraph 8.
   ___ Did you see that TV program?
   ___ I have the program from the game.
   ✓ Program the robot to make lunch.

Working with Words

Add **-ly** to the words in parentheses to complete each sentence below. Change the spelling of the base word if necessary.

1. The plane arrived ___safely___. (safe)
2. The regulations were ___strictly___ enforced. (strict)
3. The parachute opened ___automatically___ (automatic)
4. They want to be ___completely___ fair with each other. (complete)

Write the compound words from the story that have these meanings.

5. not having ___without___
   (Par. 2)
6. bag to carry clothes ___suitcase___
   (Par. 10)

Reading and Thinking

1. Write a sentence that summarizes wha air traffic controllers do.
   ___They regulate airplane movements to___
   ___keep safe distances between aircraft.___
   (Answers may vary.)

2. Do you think flying will be more safe less safe in the future? Explain.
   ___(Answers will vary.)___

3. Check the most likely reason the auth had for writing this story.
   ✓ to explain what air traffic controllers do
   ___ to tell why Pat's parents worry
   ___ to explain how safety equipment works

Learning to Study

The communication between pilot and controller is not hard to figure out if you know what the words mean.

In paragraph 11, Pat calls the Columb control tower. She then identifies her plan Vista, and the aircraft number N9857V. T words *November* and *Victor* stand for aircr call letters N and V. Pat ends her message with the word *over*, which means she is waiting for a response.

Read this radio message and then answer the questions below.

"Boston Tower Control, Vista Echo two fo Mike. Permission to land, over."

1. What airport is the pilot calling?
   ___Boston___

2. What are the call letters and numbers the plane? ___E 24 M___

3. What does the pilot want? ___to land___

Knowing the Words

Write the words from the story that have the meanings below.

1. changes ___alterations___
   (Par. 1)
2. weather scientist ___meteorologist___
   (Par. 1)
3. always ___constantly___
   (Par. 2)
4. part of a whole ___factor___
   (Par. 5)
5. met by chance ___encountered___
   (Par. 7)

Write the words from the story that are represented by these abbreviations.

6. Can. ___Canada___
   (Par. 1)
7. OH ___Ohio___
   (Par. 1)
8. Sept. ___September___
   (Par. 1)
9. hrs. ___hours___
   (Par. 2)
10. inf. ___information___
    (Par. 4)
11. wt. ___weight___
    (Par. 6)

Working with Words

Add **-er**, **-ly**, or **-y** to each word below. Then write the best word to complete each sentence.

constant   storm   hard   unexpected   cold

1. We are ___constantly___ in search of better weather information.
2. Wind can make a plane ___harder___ to control than if there were no wind.
3. The planes were grounded because the weather was too ___stormy___.
4. The weather in Maine was ___colder___ than the weather in Georgia.
5. A wind came up ___unexpectedly___ and caused the plane to bounce.

Reading and Thinking

1. Why must weather conditions be watched constantly? ___They are important___ ___for flight safety and can change at any time.___
   (Answers may vary.)

2. Check the most likely conclusion you can make after reading this story.
   ___ Meteorologists have training like that of pilots.
   ✓ Weather watching is serious business.
   ___ Weather experts use just a few techniques to make decisions.

Write the word that best completes each sentence.

3. We had to wait before taking off until weather ___conditions___ improved.
   meteorologists   conditions   visibility

4. They had to make ___alterations___ in their plans after hearing the report.
   alterations   directions   factors

Learning to Study

Read this weather report and then answer the questions below.

- Partly to mostly cloudy today
- Highs 24°–30° (F)
- Cloudy tonight with snow accumulating less than one inch
- Lows mostly in the 20s
- Chance of snow 35% tonight
- Winds west to northwest 15 to 20 mph

1. When might snow fall? ___tonight___
2. What is the chance that snow will fall? ___35%___
3. Will the temperature be above freezing during this time? ___no___

Knowing the Words

Write the words from the story that have the meanings below.

1. noble ___dignified___
   (Par. 1)
2. bother ___annoyance___
   (Par. 3)
3. roughly and strongly ___violently___
   (Par. 6)
4. got back ___regained___
   (Par. 10)
5. severe wind caused by a violent thunderstorm ___wind shear___
   (Par. 12)

Write the words from the story that are synonyms (words that have the same or nearly the same meaning) for these words.

6. postponement ___delay___
   (Par. 3)
7. dazed ___stunned___
   (Par. 8)
8. objection ___protest___
   (Par. 11)

In each row below, circle the three words that are related.

9. (jolt) (bounce) (thud) race
10. (departure) (leave) pre-flight (takeoff)

11. Check the correct meaning of the metaphor, *the plane that had become a mad dog*, from paragraph 7.
    ___ The plane turned into a wild dog.
    ✓ The plane was out of control.

Working with Words

Write the open or closed compound words from the story that are formed by adding words to these words.

1. came ___overcame___
   (Par. 5)
2. coaster ___roller coaster___
   (Par. 10)
3. where ___nowhere___
   (Par. 11)
4. shear ___wind shear___
   (Par. 12)

Reading and Thinking

1. Check the most likely reason the author had for writing this story.
   ✓ to entertain
   ___ to persuade

2. Check the word that best describes the mood of this story.
   ✓ suspenseful   ___ serious
   ___ humorous   ___ romantic

3. Check the things that show that Pat and Charlie were frightened.
   ✓ Their hearts were racing.
   ___ Charlie was catching a bad cold.
   ___ They were annoyed with the delay.
   ✓ They gasped in unison.

4. Check the words below that describe the flying weather in this story.
   ✓ stormy   ___ sunny
   ✓ rainy   ✓ windy
   ___ hot   ___ cold

Learning to Study

Study this weather table for the first days of March, and then answer the questions below.

March Sun Data			Temperature Extremes			
Date	Sunrise	Sunset	High	Year	Low	Year
1	7:05	6:23	65	1972	-2	1967
2	7:04	6:24	70	1976	0	1980
3	7:02	6:25	75	1974	0	1943
4	7:01	6:26	78	1946	-1	1943

1. Are the days getting shorter or longer? ___longer___
2. In what year was the temperature coldest on March 3? ___1943___
3. When is sunset on March 2? ___6:24 P.M.___

Knowing the Words

Write the words from the story that have the meanings below.

1. quickly looked over ___scanned___
   (Par. 1)
2. rough ___choppy___
   (Par. 1)
3. examples or cases ___instances___
   (Par. 5)
4. a happening ___occurrence___
   (Par. 9)
5. not certain ___unpredictable___
   (Par. 10)

In each row below, circle the two words that are related.

6. (disappeared) (vanished) abandoned
7. discovered (mysterious) (weird)

8. Check the sentence in which *course* has the same meaning as in paragraph 1.
   ___ Of course we will go with you.
   ___ What math course should I take?
   ✓ That course will get us there.

Working with Words

Add a prefix or a suffix from the list below to each word to form a new word. You may have to change the spelling of the base word before adding a suffix.

dis-   -ly   -y   -able

1. firm ___firmly___
2. mysterious ___mysteriously___
3. predict ___predictable___
4. cover ___discover___
5. chop ___choppy___
6. appear ___disappear___
7. creep ___creepy___
8. complete ___completely___
9. explain ___explainable___
10. spook ___spooky___

Reading and Thinking

Write **F** for fact or **O** for opinion before each statement below.

1. ___F___ Five bombers disappeared in 1945.
2. ___O___ Storms caused the disappearances.
3. ___O___ The Bermuda Triangle is a mysterious place.
4. ___F___ Navigation instruments can be affected by the weather.

5. Check the sequence that shows how Charlie's attitude about the Bermuda Triangle changed throughout the story.
   ✓ from humorous to serious to humorous
   ___ from serious to humorous to serious
   ___ from mysterious to humorous to serious

Learning to Study

Look at this map, and then answer the questions below.

1. Based on Pat's description in paragraph 3, draw lines around the area called the Bermuda Triangle.

2. What group of islands lies within the Bermuda Triangle? ___Bahama Islands___

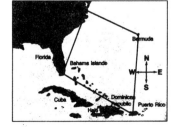

Knowing the Words

Write the words from the story that have the meanings below.

1. to be real or alive ___exist___
   (Par. 3)
2. story ___account___
   (Par. 4)
3. great excitement ___hysteria___
   (Par. 5)
4. sensible ___logical___
   (Par. 6)
5. shooting stars ___meteors___
   (Par. 6)

Drop the prefix from each word below to write the words that are antonyms (words that mean the opposite).

6. unidentified ___identified___
7. illogical ___logical___
8. insecurity ___security___
9. unreliable ___reliable___

10. Write a **7** before the sentence in which *account* has the same meaning as in paragraph 7. Write a **5** before the sentence in which *account* has the same meaning as in paragraph 5.
    ___5___ We gave the full account.
    ___7___ We could not account for the missing money.

Working with Words

Rewrite each phrase below. Use possessive forms.

1. the explanation of Charlie ___Charlie's explanation___
2. the explanation of the scientist ___the scientist's explanation___
3. the explanations of the scientists ___the scientists' explanations___

Reading and Thinking

1. Check the phrase that best expresses the main idea of this story.
   ___ a radio broadcast
   ✓ a discussion of UFOs
   ___ a scientist's study

2. Why was there mass hysteria in 1938 after a radio broadcast?
   ___People thought Martians had landed.___
   (Answers may vary.)

Write the word that best completes each sentence.

3. They saw some ___evidence___ of a crime.
   philosophy   evidence   security

4. They ___investigated___ the report.
   unidentified   investigated   frightened

Learning to Study

1. Check each reference you might use to find out more on UFOs.
   ✓ encyclopedia   ___ dictionary
   ✓ card catalog   ___ almanac
   ✓ *Readers' Guide*   ___ atlas

Read these outline headings for a story on UFOs and answer the questions below.

I. Daytime sightings
II. Fictional accounts
III. Radar sightings

2. Which item does not belong in the story?
   ___II. Fictional accounts___

3. Check the items that could be included in this story.
   ✓ face-to-face encounters
   ✓ nighttime sightings
   ___ the Bermuda Triangle

Knowing the Words

Write the words from the story that have the meanings below.

1. before the usual time ___premature___
   (Par. 3)
2. an influence ___inspiration___
   (Par. 4)
3. interested in ___inclined___
   (Par. 6)
4. changed from one to the other ___converted___
   (Par. 9)
5. Check the correct meaning of the idiom *caught their eyes* from paragraph 2.
   ___ grabbed their eyeballs
   _✓_ got their attention
6. Check the correct meaning of the idiom *bitten by the flying bug* in paragraph 9.
   _✓_ really wanted to fly
   ___ bitten by a flying insect

Working with Words

Write the words from the story that have the given prefixes and that come from these foreign base words.

1. **in-** + *spirare*
   meaning "to breathe" ___inspiration___
   (Par. 4)
2. **en-** + *corage*,
   meaning "courage" ___encouraged___
   (Par. 4)
3. **in-** + *struere*,
   meaning "to build" ___instructor___
   (Par. 5)
4. **in-** + *clinare*,
   meaning "to lean" ___inclined___
   (Par. 6)

Write the words from the story that have the suffix **-ly** and that are formed from these base words.

5. mechanical ___mechanically___
6. short ___shortly___

Reading and Thinking

1. Why did William J. Powell establish a flight school?
   ___African Americans were denied flying lessons.___
   (Answers may vary.)

Write **C** before statements that describe Cornelius Coffey. Write **L** before statements that describe Charles Lindbergh in the story on page 32. Write **C/L** before statements that describe both.

2. _L_ He got a lot of publicity.
3. _C/L_ His life spanned flight history.
4. _C/L_ He was mechanically inclined.

Write **T** before the statements that are true. Write **F** before those that are false.

5. _F_ African-American women never became pilots.
6. _T_ In 1932, James Banning made a transcontinental flight.
7. _T_ Many African Americans wanted to fly planes.
8. _F_ Until 1964, African-Americans had to go to France to get flying lessons.

Learning to Study

Complete this partial outline of African-American aviators and their accomplishments.

I. Bessie Coleman
   A. ___first African-American woman with pilot's license___
   B. ___was an inspiration to many flyers___
II. William J. Powell
   A. ___was an engineer___
   B. ___established Coleman Aeroclub___
III. James Herman Banning
   A. ___chief pilot at Coleman School___
   B. ___made a 1932 transcontinental flight___
   (Answers may vary.)

Knowing the Words

Write the words from the story that have the meanings below.

1. something left out ___exception___
   (Par. 1)
2. genuine ___authentic___
   (Par. 1)
3. objects used as guides ___landmarks___
   (Par. 3)
4. balloon or airship fliers ___aeronauts___
   (Par. 5)
5. Check the sentence in which *past* has the same meaning as in paragraph 5.
   ___ I could not see past the trees.
   ___ In the past twenty minutes, the phone has rung six times.
   _✓_ In the past, we would not have found the error.

Write the words from the story that are antonyms (words that mean the opposite) of these words.

6. floor ___ceiling___
   (Par. 1)
7. above ___beneath___
   (Par. 1)
8. unfamiliar ___familiar___
   (Par. 3)
9. apart ___together___
   (Par. 9)
10. dull ___bright___
    (Par. 17)

Working with Words

Write the compound words from the story that are formed by adding to these words.

1. taking ___breathtaking___
   (Par. 1)
2. open ___open-cockpit___
   (Par. 3)
3. marks ___landmarks___
   (Par. 3)
4. end ___weekend___
   (Par. 8)

Reading and Thinking

1. Check the phrase that best expresses the main idea of this story.
   ___ famous planes
   ___ Pat's friends
   _✓_ the past, present, and future
2. Check the most likely conclusion you can make about the navigation system of the open-cockpit mail planes.
   _✓_ There were few instruments.
   ___ They had radio-controlled system
   ___ They used radar for navigation.
3. Check the conclusions you can make based on the fact that Pat was "walking on air" after she saw Ross.
   _✓_ She was pleased to see Ross.
   ___ She was enjoying the exhibit.
   ___ She had lost a lot of weight.
   ___ Her feet were sore.
   _✓_ She was happy that Ross wanted go to dinner with her.
4. Do you think Pat and Ross will contin to see each other? Explain.
   _____
   (Answers will vary.)

Learning to Study

Read this dictionary entry. Then write the parts of the entry that are requested below

break / bräk / *vb* **broke**; **bro ken 1** to suddenly separate; SHATTER, CUT **2** to fail to keep **3** to crush

1. entry word ___break___
2. part of speech abbreviation ___vb___
3. irregular forms ___broke; broken___
4. respelling ___/bräk/___

Checking Understanding

Test 1   These exercises are to be completed after reading the story on page 10.

1. Check two sentences that are true. (2)
   ___ Pterodactyls were large birds.
   _✓_ Pterodactyl fossils have been found.
   _✓_ Pat and Charlie were heading north in their plane.
2. National Airport is in ___Washington, D.C.___
3. Check another good title for this story.
   ___ Fossils of West Texas
   ___ Prehistoric Animals
   _✓_ A Model of a Flying Reptile
4. Why was the model tested?
   ___to see if a large animal could fly___

5. Pterodactyls lived in ___prehistoric___ times.
6. How were the model's wings powered?
   ___by electric motors___
7. Number these events in the order in which they happen in the story.
   _3_ Pat called the control tower.
   _1_ Charlie saw the reptile.
   _4_ Frank told them about the model.
   _6_ Charlie made a joke about birds.
   _5_ Pat said she had been startled.
   _2_ Pat saw the reptile below them.
8. Write two things these reptiles did to fly. (2) ___moved their wings; shifted weight___

Number of Words Read per Minute [ ]

Test Score (Possible Score–10) [ ]

Test 2   These exercises are to be completed after reading the story on page 30.

1. Check another good title for this story.
   ___ Overnight Fame
   _✓_ An Extraordinary Person
   ___ Around the World
2. Becoming a pilot was hard for Earhart because ___there were few women pilots___
3. Earhart felt she did not deserve overnight fame because ___she had just been a passenger___
4. Write two records that Earhart set. (2)
   ___first woman to fly solo across the Atlantic, the U.S., and the Pacific___
   (Accept any two of these answers.)

5. Check two sentences that are true. (2)
   ___ Earhart had average flying skills.
   ___ Earhart flew around the world.
   _✓_ Earhart was calm under pressure.
   _✓_ Earhart wasn't immediately accepted by other pilots.
6. Fred Noonan was Earhart's ___navigator___
7. Write one possible reason for Earhart's disappearance. ___engine trouble; ran out of fuel; captured by Japanese___
   (Accept any one of these answers.)
8. Why is Earhart's story a mystery?
   ___No one knows what happened to her.___

Number of Words Read per Minute [ ]

Test Score (Possible Score–10) [ ]

Test 3   These exercises are to be completed after reading the story on page 44.

1. Number these events in the order in which they happened in the story.
   _2_ Jane explained hang gliders.
   _3_ Charlotte joked about Pat's fear.
   _4_ Jane took off in her hang glider.
   _1_ Charlotte persuaded Pat to learn about hang gliding.
   _5_ Pat saw a young girl and an older man try hang gliding.
   _6_ Pat agreed to try hang gliding.
2. Check two sentences that are true. (2)
   _✓_ Pat had not flown in a sailplane.
   _✓_ A hang glider is triangular.
   ___ A new kind of airfoil was patented in the 1950s.
   ___ Pat was fond of hang gliding.

3. Write two things that should be worn be safe while hang gliding. (2)
   ___boots, helmet, long pants___
   (Accept any two of these answers.)
4. Check another good title for the story.
   ___ The Wind Is Our Friend
   _✓_ Pat's Hang Gliding Lesson
   ___ An Afternoon in Virginia
5. Many people began hang gliding after ___someone patented an airfoil___
6. Hang gliders are steered by ___control bar___
7. Jane ___ hang gliding.
   ___ fears ___ dislikes _✓_ enjoys
8. Hang gliders become airborne when ___the sail fills with air___

Number of Words Read per Minute [ ]

Test Score (Possible Score–10) [ ]

Test 4   These exercises are to be completed after reading the story on page 78.

1. In what ocean is the Bermuda Triangle? ___Atlantic___
2. Why is the Bermuda Triangle weird?
   ___Planes and ships have vanished there.___
3. Write two reasons why planes vanish in the Bermuda Triangle. (2)
   ___winds; engine trouble; lost in a storm___
   (Accept any two of these answers.)
4. Pat refused to be ___.
   ___ hungry ___ calm _✓_ jinxed
5. Planes could run out of fuel in storms because ___they could get lost___

6. Check two sentences that are true. (2)
   _✓_ The Bermuda Triangle has four sides.
   ___ All planes vanish in the Triangle.
   _✓_ More than fifty planes and ships have been lost in the Triangle.
7. Check another good title for this story.
   _✓_ Mystery in the Atlantic Ocean
   ___ Bermuda Onion for Lunch
   ___ Frozen Foods for Bermuda
8. The Gulf Stream could cause trouble because ___it is unpredictable___

Number of Words Read per Minute [ ]

Test Score (Possible Score–10) [ ]